IMAGES
of America

THE OWENS VALLEY

Beautiful Owens Valley
Inyo County] "The INLAND EMPIRE" [California

—— AN INYO COUNTY HAYING SCENE ——

That Owens Valley is the ideal locality for the homeseeker, is demonstrated by the great variety of its productions, its splendid climate, good schools, churches, and progressive hospitable people. All crops being raised by irrigation, and the irrigation systems owned by farmers using the water, expense is kept down to the minimum, and such a thing as drouth is unknown. Hay and grain are great revenue-producers. Alfalfa grown for hay or seed always bring good returns. The new broad-gauge railroad now nearly complete from Los Angeles through the valley to Northern and Eastern points, guarantees to the rancher additional markets for all products as well as quick service. If you are looking for a home in a land where you have sunshine instead of rain, fogs, drouth and malaria, Beautiful Owens Valley will bear your closest investigation.

For further information, address

BOARD OF SUPERVISORS . . . . . . INDEPENDENCE, CALIFORNIA
CHAMBER OF COMMERCE . . . . BISHOP, CALIFORNIA
UNITED STATES LAND OFFICE . . . . INDEPENDENCE, CALIFORNIA

As the Los Angeles Aqueduct neared completion in 1913, Owens Valley residents remained hopefully optimistic for their future. Agents advertised land for sale and circulated "booster" literature, including this magazine supplement that extolls the valley's scenery, climate, farming potential, and abundant water. (Eastern California Museum.)

ON THE COVER: The Sierra Nevada forms the backdrop for this photograph from about 1909 of workers completing the diversion gates that will turn the Owens River into the Los Angeles Aqueduct. (Los Angeles Department of Water and Power.)

IMAGES
of America

THE OWENS VALLEY

Jane Wehrey

ARCADIA
PUBLISHING

Published by Arcadia Publishing
Charleston, South Carolina

Library of Congress Control Number: 2012937704

For all general information, please contact Arcadia Publishing:
Telephone 843-853-2070
Fax 843-853-0044
E-mail sales@arcadiapublishing.com
For customer service and orders:
Toll-Free 1-888-313-2665

Visit us on the Internet at www.arcadiapublishing.com

In this view of the Owens Valley looking south from Bishop Airport in the early 1950s, Bishop pilot and photographer Robert Symons has captured cloud formations that appear when airflow over the Sierra Nevada creates the powerful lifting currents known as the "Sierra Wave." (Patricia Symons Rowbottom collection.)

CONTENTS

ACKNOWLEDGMENTS

My gratitude goes first to the staff of the Eastern California Museum in Independence: Jon Klusmire, director; Roberta Harlan, curator of collections; and Heather Todd, museum assistant. As custodians of a remarkable photographic archive, they have generously supported this project in many ways.

Thank you, also, to the following people who supplied images and information: Anh-Thu Pham, Dr. Paul Soifer, and Angela Tatum, Los Angeles Department of Water and Power; Pamela Vaughan, Laws Museum; David Welle and students, Deep Springs College; Elizabeth Babcock, Maturango Museum; Alan Miyatake, Toyo Miyatake Studio; Erik Leitch and Mary Daniel, Owens Valley Radio Observatory; Dennis Burke and Brian Norden, Southern Pacific Narrow Gauge Historical Society; Maggie Wolfe, Bristlecone Chapter, California Native Plant Society; Melanie Hubbard, Department of Archives and Special Collections, William Hannon Library, Loyola Marymount University; Nancy Masters, Inyo County Library; Loma Karklins, California Institute of Technology; Chris Langley, Inyo County film commissioner, Lone Pine Museum of Film History; Alisa Lynch, chief of interpretation, Manzanar National Historic Site; artist Susan Holgate, photographers Kenneth Babione and Michel Wehrey, and photographer/filmmaker Michael Pietrobon.

June Bagwell, Bruce Branson, Irma Cline, Jean Crispin, Gordon Hastings, Bruce and Elsie Ivey, Mary Mairs, Kathleen New, Evelyn Mae Nikolaus, Ernestine Perez, Tom Poole, and Patricia Symons Rowbottom enthusiastically dug into their photo collections and memories for images and information. I am grateful also to Donna Stanger, and especially to John Poultney and Arcadia Publishing staff and acquisitions editors Jeff Ruetsche, Amy Perryman, and Elizabeth Bray.

For over 150 years, explorers, scientists, historians, journalists, photographers, artists, and website creators have documented the Owens Valley's landscape, history, and people, most in far greater depth and detail than this photographic album permits. As sources of information and inspiration, their contributions have been invaluable. Unless otherwise indicated, images in *The Owens Valley* are used courtesy of the Eastern California Museum, County of Inyo, in Independence, California.

At the dedication of the fourth and present Inyo County Courthouse on April 10, 1922, in Independence, all native-born county residents present that day assembled on the courthouse steps for this photograph taken by Lone Pine photographer Allen Ramsey.

INTRODUCTION

To come to the Owens Valley is to be captivated by a landscape of bold beauty, where towering alpine peaks, deep desert canyons, and sweeping vistas of light and shadow inspire awe and invite discovery of the "long brown land," and "land of little rain" of author Mary Austin's desert writings. To the west, the Sierra Nevada's sheer eastern flank rises nearly two miles from the 4,000-foot valley floor. Small towns strung along its nearly 100-mile length are dwarfed by jagged granite crests that include Mount Whitney, at 14,497 feet, the highest point in the contiguous United States. Only 90 miles distant, beyond the barren White-Inyo Range to the east is Badwater in Death Valley, North America's lowest place, at 282 feet below sea level.

Between them, the deep, narrow trough of the Owens Valley marks a rare confluence of biogeographic regions—the Great Basin, Mojave Desert, and Sierra Nevada—where the geologic features, climate, and plant and animal life of each overlap in a remarkable diversity of life and landforms. Sand dunes are within view of snow, gnarled 4,000-year-old trees of the Bristlecone Pine Forest cling to the White Mountains' high-elevation slopes, and the forces of earthquakes, glaciers, wind, and water are clearly visible. Lying in the Sierra Nevada rain shadow, the valley receives just six inches annually; its abundant water instead flows down from the Sierra's snowfields in dozens of crystalline streams. Historian John Walton has described it as "a clearly delineated space of human scale ringed nearly around by an awesome geography . . . compact, yet ineffably spacious." Its native Paiute called it Inyo, "dwelling place of the Great Spirit."

Today, most people enter the valley via US Highway 395, the iconic artery that began as an Indian trail and now brings millions of tourists to a region that was the last in modern California to be settled. Untouched by 18th-century Spanish colonizers, it was known only to ancestors of today's Owens Valley Paiute until 1834, when explorer Joseph Walker became the first recorded white visitor. By 1845, John C. Fremont's third expedition had named the valley, its river, and its large saline lake for expedition member Richard Owens. Miners came first, starting in 1860, to claim the Inyo Mountains' rich deposits of silver and gold, and cattlemen followed, driving stock from Central California. White dwellings appeared at present-day Independence, and Samuel Bishop and his wife, the valley's first white woman, established the San Francis Ranch near where the valley's largest town bears their name.

Since then, the interplay of landscape and human activity has produced an Owens Valley history as dramatic as the land itself. Like most of the West, it was a meeting ground of diverse peoples—Mexicans, Chinese, Canadians, Northern Europeans, settlers from the Northeast and Midwest—whose dreams of prosperity and new beginnings brought many into open conflict with the native Paiute—and with one another. Colorful mining camps at Bend City, Chrysopolis, and Cerro Gordo attracted fortune-seekers and stimulated agriculture, stock raising, logging, and freighting. The steamers *Bessie Brady* and *Molly Stevens* transported Cerro Gordo's wealth across Owens Lake, and the 1883 Carson & Colorado Railroad opened the isolated valley from the north. Farmers and stockmen put down roots in outposts at Lone Pine, Independence, Big Pine, and Bishop, and state and federal governments assisted settlement in surveys of land later offered free under federal land laws, and in the presence of a US Cavalry unit sent to mediate white-Indian conflicts. Inyo County, formed in 1866, placed its county seat at Independence. As mining waned in the late 1800s, the Owens Valley became largely agrarian, and although a large reservoir and needed rail link to Southern California were still missing, residents' heady visions of an Owens Valley agricultural empire carried forward into a new century.

The century-long presence of the City of Los Angeles as water exporter and principal landowner is indisputably the Owens Valley's best-known history. Construction on the Los Angeles Aqueduct started in 1908; and in the decades that followed, a sparsely-populated desert valley and rapidly growing urban center were brought together in an epic saga of colliding rural-urban values, conflicting visions of resource allocation, and uses and misuses of political power. On a national and international stage, the aqueduct remains a controversial symbol of the social, economic, and environmental issues associated with large-scale water transfers in arid lands. The telling and refashioning of the story over decades has generated its own parallel controversy. Pivotal for both valley and city was Pres. Theodore Roosevelt's support for the project, which cited the "few" in the Owens Valley whose interests "must unfortunately be disregarded in view of the infinitely greater interest to be served by putting the water in Los Angeles." In the period of hopeful calm and plentiful water that followed the aqueduct's opening in 1913, Owens Valley agricultural production increased, but Los Angeles' exponential growth continued to cast a long shadow on the Owens Valley future. By the mid-1920s, the Owens Valley "water wars" were under way in earnest, as Los Angeles returned to buy more land and water rights and bitterness within the valley often matched that directed against the city.

No less dramatic were the years after 1927, when the valley languished in depression and civic leaders joined together to enlist Los Angeles as a partner in the region's rebirth as a tourist and recreation mecca. In 1940, one million people traveled into the valley, most from Southern California. Cattle and hay production continued as strong components of the economy, along with new extractive industries that included high-grade tungsten taken from Union Carbide's Pine Creek mine near Bishop. Following World War II, tourism increased, and with it service sector employment. By 1970, tourism revenue was double that of ranching, mining, and logging combined, and in 1980 agricultural occupations comprised just three per cent of workers, down from 40 per cent before 1930.

The transformation from agrarian to service economy brought social changes as well. Nineteenth-century residents of the valley's towns had coped with their isolation by creating networks of civic involvement and community traditions such as Bishop's Harvest Festivals and Lone Pine's September 16 celebration of its Mexican community's heritage. Community bonds loosened as the roads that brought tourists into the valley also took residents away, for recreation, education, and employment. In the decades since, retirees, new ethnic groups, and urban transplants have joined descendants of the valley's pioneer families in new traditions and civic responsibilities.

A landscape long valued for its mineral wealth and agricultural potential, and more recently for the tourism dollars to be made from its scenery, came to be viewed in the early 1970s as a fragile natural environment requiring watchful stewardship. Environmental damage related to increased groundwater pumping set off a new 19-year Owens Valley water war with Los Angeles in 1972, fought this time in the courts. Started in 2000 in response to an air quality mandate, Los Angeles' $1 billion Owens Lake Dust Mitigation project has treated 40 square miles of lakebed dried by aqueduct water diversions, significantly reducing dust and airborne pollutants.

With fewer than 20,000 people and less than two percent of land in private ownership, the Owens Valley is an anomaly in urbanized California. If its landscape appears today strangely untouched by a human presence traceable back at least 10,000 years, it is because, as historian John Walton points out, it has been instead "touched so often," by a complex and colorful past.

One
DWELLERS IN A
LONELY LAND

Early impressions of the Owens Valley were as varied as the landscape itself. "Worthless to the white man, both in soil and climate," state surveyor A.W. Von Schmidt declared in 1855. In 1864, William Brewer recorded, "This valley sees but little rain, but where streams come down from the Sierra . . . great meadows of green grass occur." This view is looking north from near Lone Pine. (Author's collection.)

Owen's Lake, Cal. 13t.

The Owens River carries the water of more than 40 Sierra streams into Owens Lake, a saline sink without outlet. "Not a pleasant piece of water," miners reported in 1867. The lake is seen in this view (above) looking southeast in the early 1900s, before agricultural and aqueduct diversions dried it completely. Author Mary Austin, writing around the same time, describes "a bitter lake, cupped round with desertness." Evidence of human habitation dates to at least 10,000 years ago and includes the hundreds of petroglyphs, or rock art, found throughout the valley. This one (left) is on the volcanic tableland north of Bishop. While the carvings' symbols and designs may vary stylistically by site, their exact age, origins, and purpose remain a mystery. Stone circles, obsidian chips, and seed-grinding rocks are usually attributed to more recent ancestors of the present Owens Valley Paiute.

As they encountered early white visitors, inhabitants of the valley called themselves *numu*, or "people." Whites later called them Paiute, for their likeness to other northern Great Basin groups. Based in small communities of tule shelters similar to this one below, they followed a seasonal subsistence cycle of hunting game, collecting insect larvae, and harvesting grasses, tubers, and pine nuts—a winter staple. To supplement their diet, they diverted streams to irrigate cultivated plots of native plants. In 1855, the surveyor A.W. Von Schmidt observed "about 1000 Indians . . . and they are a fine looking set of men." US Army captain J.W. Davidson later reported, "[The Indians'] true character is that of an interesting, peaceful, industrious people." At right, in a 1914 photograph by Andrew Forbes, Truman Buff, an Owens Valley Paiute, holds his brother Philip in a traditional cradleboard.

As the 1849 Gold Rush waned, rumors of new strikes in the Owens Valley led prospectors and entrepreneurs over the Sierra. The New World Mining and Exploration Company located a gold-bearing ledge southeast of present-day Independence in 1860. In the following years, miners filed hundreds of claims along the Inyo Mountains' west flank, including Chrysopolis, San Carlos, Golden Era, and Silver Cloud. The Eclipse Mine, later called the Brown Monster, was among the most productive. Workers are seen above after it became the Reward Mine in the late 1800s. Cattlemen appeared in the valley starting in 1861, driving herds from drought-parched Southern and Central California to the Owens Valley's lush meadows. Many stayed, claimed land, and profited from selling beef and grain to mining camps. The Calvert Ranch, pictured below, was north of Independence at Tibbetts Station, later called Aberdeen.

The effects of grazing cattle on Indian food sources were immediate and devastating. Facing starvation, Indians raided cattle herds, whites retaliated, and loss of life escalated. Settlers and miners fled the valley, and those who stayed requested protection. On July 4, 1862, a unit of the US 2nd Cavalry, California Volunteers, raised the flag over a crude outpost on Oak Creek and called it Camp Independence. A fragile truce gave way to more bloodshed, and in July 1863, soldiers removed nearly 1,000 Indians from the valley in a brutal 200-mile march south across the desert to the San Sebastian Reservation at Fort Tejon. With the valley seemingly secure, the cavalry departed, but as homesteaders and exiled Indians gradually returned, new violence erupted. Soldiers reoccupied the fort in 1865; it is seen above in the 1870s. Below, Paiute Mary Lent sorts unshelled pine nuts.

North Carolina native Andrew Bell arrived in the Owens Valley in 1862 and later built a flour mill at Oak Creek on property that stayed in the Bell family until 2010. Bell employed Indians living nearby and supplied flour to the Fort Independence military post. Farmers from all over the valley brought grain to be milled and often spent the night at the Bells' home. The mill closed in 1923, after a violent windstorm partially destroyed it.

Fort Independence brought order and stability to the valley's often lawless mining camps and pioneer communities. A welcome market for local beef and grain, it was also a lively center of social life for neighboring towns. Rebuilt after the 1872 earthquake, the post was considered among the most beautiful in the West. White frame homes and buildings surrounded the parade ground, seen here before the fort closed in 1877. (California State Military Museum.)

Before settlement began, thousands of miners passed through the valley on their way to Nevada's silver camps, but by 1863, according to historian W. A. Chalfant, permanent settlers were arriving "at a lively rate," most of them from the south on the Los Angeles-Aurora Road first used by the miners. As seen on this 1864 map, mining camps at Owensville, Chrysopolis, San Carlos, and Bend City were the valley's first large towns. By 1870, they had nearly disappeared.

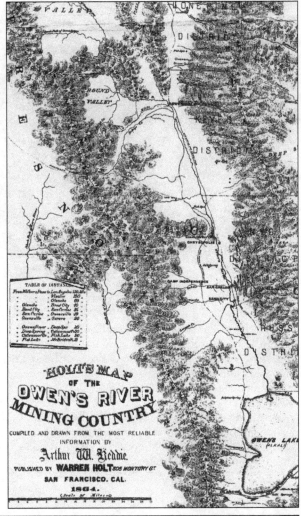

An 1871 state law authorizing private citizens to construct and operate toll roads helped open remote areas to mining and trade. The 32-mile Deep Springs Valley Toll Road, built into Nevada from near Big Pine in 1873, operated until 1921. At the First Spring tollhouse, seen here, builder J.S. Broder collected 5¢ for sheep and goats and $1 for a wagon and two animals. (Bruce Branson collection.)

15

Mexican prospectors found silver and lead deposits in the Inyo Mountains high above Owens Lake in 1865 and called the strike Cerro Gordo, or "fat hill." By 1870, fortune-seekers had filed more than 1,000 claims, and Cerro Gordo was the richest silver mining district in California. San Francisco businessman Mortimer Belshaw brought financing and modern smelting methods. To squeeze out competitors, he built the legendary Yellow Grade Road to the mines and collected tolls as wagons hauled supplies and equipment up eight miles of steep, rocky track from the valley below and returned loaded with heavy bullion. After Belshaw joined with his competitor Victor Beaudry in the Union Mining Company, the two controlled most of "fat hill." Below, early freight wagons to Los Angeles could not keep up with the bullion output, and stacks of the glistening bars grew alongside the smelters.

By 1869, Cerro Gordo had over 1,500 people and only a semblance of law and order. Newspaperman P.A. Chalfant called it "a shooting gallery." Lone Pine saloon operator Lola Travis had moved to Inyo County in 1867 from Chihuahua, Mexico, and later established her dance hall and red-light house at Cerro Gordo on property owned by a gentleman friend. Women owned many of Cerro Gordo's pleasure establishments. Down the street from Lola's dance hall, Maggie Moore operated another brothel known as Waterfalls, and Mary Morales had a saloon nearby. As her wealth grew Travis expanded her businesses to Panamint City and Darwin, purchased property and educations for her four children and younger siblings, and indulged her liking for fast horses and expensive dresses. A fire at Cerro Gordo in 1880 originated at Waterfalls and took out most of the main street. Travis lost her brothel and with it her fortune. She eventually settled in Bakersfield, where a third marriage brought the respectability she had always longed to have. She died in 1912 at age 75.

Cerro Gordo's output of at least $15 million was the largest in California history. Most of that wealth went elsewhere, however. More significant for the Owens Valley's future was the transportation operation of Los Angeles freighter Remi Nadeau (left). By 1874, with 80 teams of 14 to 16 mules each pulling three huge wagons on a round-the-clock schedule, Nadeau could haul up to 18 tons of silver bullion daily to Los Angeles for shipment to San Francisco. The wagons returned loaded with food, spirits, clothing, and equipment, all from Los Angeles–area farmers and wholesalers. That huge infusion of capital transformed Los Angeles from a sleepy backwater town to a booming metropolis-in-the-making. An 1872 *Los Angeles News* article declares, "What Los Angeles is, is mainly due to [Cerro Gordo]. It is the silver cord that binds our existence." (Below, Laws Museum and Historic Site.)

Remi Nadeau's Cerro Gordo Freighting Company dominated the eastern California freighting business between 1873 and 1882. To feed his 1,000 or more mules, he raised hay and barley in Los Angeles and purchased feed from Owens Valley ranchers. Above, one of Nadeau's teams hauls a load of hay from John Shepherd's ranch at George's Creek, possibly to one of the freight way stations established at 13-to-20-mile intervals along the 230-mile "Bullion Trail" to Los Angeles. Shepherd, seen at right with his wife, Margaret, was among the valley's most successful and respected ranchers. The family's elegant home, built in 1872, was an Owens Valley showplace. Together with his Indian workers, Shepherd built and operated a toll wagon road from Darwin into Panamint Valley, opening the area to mining and stage travel.

Indians returning to the valley from Fort Tejon after 1863 found their food-gathering territories occupied by white settlers and their centuries-old way of life changed forever. Destitute and facing new calls for removal, they took jobs on the farms and ranches that had displaced them. Men worked as farm laborers and built roads, and women did housework for white families and winnowed grain at harvest time. Their labor soon became essential to the valley's pioneer economy. Above, Indian workers, including women, sack grain in rancher John Gorman's field south of Independence in 1904. Livestock production also employed many Indians, including cowboy Chappo Bellas (second from left, on horse), seen below working at the Lubken Ranch west of Lone Pine. Indian workers typically took the surnames of their white employers.

The northern valley's grasslands, large streams, and rich alluvial soil attracted the largest share of early homesteaders. By 1880, the Bishop area led the region in number of farms and improved acreage. In well-watered Round Valley, north of Bishop, William Roberts, a Welshman, grew mostly corn and alfalfa hay. He built this silo, reportedly the first in California and one of many later visible on the Owens Valley landscape.

Men often went ahead to claim homesteads and try farming before sending for their wives and children. Pioneers John E. and Thomas E. Jones, also from Wales, planted the area's first wheat in Round Valley in 1865. In the following years, Thomas, together with his large family, prospered selling hay, grain, fruits, and vegetables to mining camps and the Fort Independence military post. The family later operated a creamery.

William Penn Colonial Association of California

Capital Stock, $200,000
$20 per Share

✿ ✿

13,000 Acres of Fertile Fruit and Farming Land
42 Miles of Main Canals Completed

OFFICERS AND DIRECTORS

DR. W. V. COFFIN, President, Whittier, Cal.

L. M. BALDWIN, Vice-President, Whittier, Cal.

GEO. E. LITTLE, Treasurer, Whittier, Cal.

ALVA STARBUCK, Whittier, Cal.

WM. E. COX, Sec. and Gen. Mgr., Los Angeles, Cal.
1118 Savings Bank and Trust Bldg.

Despite the exodus of many homesteaders, most settlers persevered and put down permanent roots. As new arrivals claimed arid parcels far from the river, farmers organized the first cooperative ditch companies in 1878 and began digging the Bishop Creek and McNally Canals. By 1900, some 17 ditch companies managed a network of canals nearly 200 miles long that delivered irrigation water to dry lands. Above, in the foreground of this early-1900s view of the Reward Mine, the Eastside, or Inyo, Canal, started in 1887, followed the valley's eastern edge south from near Independence. At left, despite abundant irrigation water, Quaker farmers at the Southern California–based William Penn Colony struggled in the desert environment east of Lone Pine and were the first to sell to Los Angeles in 1905.

Two
CREATING COMMUNITIES

By 1870, more than 1,000 people lived in the Owens Valley. As mining declined through the next two decades, the valley economy became primarily agrarian. Farming and ranching families brought stability to fledgling towns, and new homesteaders helped form small outlying communities, including Warm Springs, Sunland, and Poleta, near the town of Bishop Creek. Teachers and children of the Warm Springs School District are seen here about 1890.

THE GREAT INYO EARTHQUAKE.

ANTONIA MONTOYA'S TRAGIC DEATH. DEATH OF MEYSAN'S CHILD. MUZINGER & LUBKEN'S BREWE

LONE PINE DURING THE CONVULSION.

The Owens Valley's early white settlements were little more than clusters of crude dwellings built of sod, rough lumber, or rocks. In the wood-scarce southern valley, Lone Pine's early residents, many of them originally from Mexico, used mainly unreinforced adobe bricks. At 2:30 a.m. on March 26, 1872, a long, deep rumbling awakened the valley, "as if the very earth was groaning in agony," recalled Independence resident Lulu Gorman. The massive earthquake, by some estimates equal in magnitude to the 1906 San Francisco quake, was among the strongest in recorded California history. Centered near Lone Pine, it destroyed nearly the entire town and collapsed brick buildings throughout the valley. The earthquake claimed 29 lives, most of them in Lone Pine, where 16 victims lie in a common grave north of town, atop the fault scarp made by this quake and others before it. The earth's fracturing created Diaz Lake south of Lone Pine and temporarily halted the Owens River's flow. This graphic in the April 21, 1872, issue of the *San Francisco Chronicle* documents eyewitness accounts of the destruction gathered by a correspondent who traveled to Lone Pine after the quake.

A solitary Jeffrey pine near an early-1860s prospectors' camp in the southern valley became the namesake for the creek nearby and a cluster of adobe dwellings downstream. The tree blew over in an 1882 windstorm, but Lone Pine grew into a multiethnic hub of commerce and transportation, supplying mining camps, ranches, and later, railroad crews and soda ash operations. As Cerro Gordo boomed in 1869, Charles and Madeleine Meysan, originally from France, opened a Lone Pine general store. Rebuilt after the 1872 earthquake, it is seen above soon after 1900, with Madeleine sitting in the chair at center and their son Felix third from the right. With fire an ever-present threat in early towns, manning a volunteer fire department was a civic obligation. Members of the Dearborn, Burkhardt, Reynolds, Skinner, Carrasco, and other pioneer families served on the 1885 Lone Pine Fire Brigade.

Silver and gold ores found in 1864 on Kearsarge Peak brought miners to the Rex Montis Mine and other high-elevation claims. High in the canyon nearby, Kearsarge City, with a population of 1,500, was the largest town in the new Inyo County until an avalanche partially destroyed it in 1867. The 10-stamp Kearsarge Mill is shown in an 1871 Wheeler Survey Expedition photograph. Below, silver and lead discoveries east of Owens Lake in 1874 made Darwin an instant boomtown with 3,500 people, 15 saloons, and a well-deserved reputation for violence. Although "respectable" women represented only a small fraction of mining camp populations, they brought a civilizing influence. Kate Bigelow, a member of Bishop High School's first graduating class, taught at the Darwin School in 1907. Mining continued intermittently through most of the 20th century. Today, around 50 people live in Darwin.

Above, Kearsarge Peak's symmetry frames Independence about 1918, with the third Inyo County Courthouse on the right and the dance pavilion on the left. The town began in 1861 as Putnam's, a stone cabin and trading post where settlers sought refuge during Indian raids. A frontier village called Little Pine had grown up around it when cattleman Thomas Edwards arrived in 1863. He bought the cabin and the adjacent land and laid out the town of Independence in 1866, naming streets for historic American men and alleyways after female relatives. The same year, officials designated the town as the county seat of newly formed Inyo County. Four courthouses have since graced its main street. The first, a brick structure, collapsed in the 1872 earthquake; the 1886 Independence fire destroyed its ornate replacement (below); and a third building remained in use until the present courthouse was completed in 1922.

Built in 1872, Irwin's Old Corner Saloon occupied the southwest corner of Edwards and Market Streets in Independence. In early communities, saloons far outnumbered fraternal lodges, but both were centers of social life—for men. "Respectable" women formed garden clubs, ladies' aid societies, and literary and drama groups. Everyone, including children, attended community potluck suppers, old-time dances, and traveling Chautauqua events.

The Independence Masonic Temple, seen here in the 1930s, replaced the first hall that Masons built after chartering Inyo Lodge No. 221 in 1872. Fraternal lodges, including the Independent Order of Good Templars, chartered at Camp Independence in 1867, rallied sentiment against lawlessness and drunkenness in early towns. Masonic organizations in particular served as leadership groups and networks of mutual aid and civic involvement in Independence, Big Pine, and Bishop. (Author's collection.)

Henry Levy and his family owned and managed the landmark Independence Hotel for more than 70 years. Seen here on the front porch, they are, from left to right, (seated) wife Mary Joseph Levy, daughter Minnie Mairs, and Henry Levy; (standing) daughters Edith Brierly and Birdie Yandell, sons Milton and Walter Levy, and daughter Lena Levy. A native of Poland, Henry established his hotel and restaurant business in 1874. After a fire on June 30, 1886, destroyed the hotel and 37 other Independence buildings, he rebuilt the same year and added more rooms later. As more travelers arrived by rail in the 1880s, Levy opened a livery stable and operated a stage to ferry passengers from Citrus (later Kearsarge) Station to Independence and back. After his death in 1924, his sons operated the hotel, restaurant, and saloon until 1945.

Many of the valley's 1,000 or more Indians lived in camps of shacks or willow shelters near the towns and ranches where they worked. The federal government formally set aside 80 acres of former military land at Fort Independence for them in 1902. In 1915–1916, executive orders established the Fort Independence Indian Reservation, the valley's first, with 356 acres. Earlier, white townspeople had organized this school for the Fort Independence Indians. Students of all ages and their teacher stand beneath the flag about 1900. Under state law, Indian children were barred from white public schools unless an Indian school was not available nearby, and while federal Indian schools were also established at Bishop and Big Pine, they did not include high school. In 1923, Indian student Alice Piper tried to enter the public high school in Big Pine and was turned away. Piper's parents challenged the exclusion law in court, and the California Supreme Court ruled in their favor, giving legal authority to the right of Indian children to attend public schools. *Piper v. Big Pine* was later cited as precedent in *Brown v. Board of Education*.

Newspapers and mail service were vital communication links in the isolated valley. On July 9, 1870, Pleasant A. Chalfant and James Parker printed the inaugural issue of Inyo County's first newspaper, the *Inyo Independent*, upstairs in Chalfant's Independence home. Above, Chalfant's son W.A. "Bill" Chalfant is seen on the right in the Bishop printing office where he and his father started that town's newspaper, the *Inyo Register*, in 1885. Inyo County's leading newspapers carried the Chalfant masthead for more than a century. The company also published magazines and local-interest books, including several written by newspaperman-turned-historian Bill (W.A.). Seen below, the Independence Post Office was established in 1866, the year the town became the Inyo County seat. Postmaster Nettie Fausel, on the left in about 1915, took over the job from her father in 1903 and handled the town's mail for 43 years.

INE. MAY. 30ᵀᴴ, 1914

Remembered by longtime resident Clarice Uhlmeyer as "a quiet country village," Big Pine is seen above on Memorial Day 1914 as women dressed in summer white walk past the Butler Hotel on Main Street toward the cemetery. Founded in 1869 to supply mines in the White-Inyo Mountains, Big Pine attracted cattlemen, farmers, and fruit growers, who named the town for the tall ponderosa pines growing nearby that supplied lumber for their homes. At left, the stately Big Pine Methodist Church, built in 1895, reflects the Midwestern roots of many town families. It remains a center of community life today. The area's earliest churches included the Baptist congregation organized in Bishop Creek in 1869 and the Independence Pioneer Methodist Church established in 1871—the oldest continuously active church in the county.

Seen here about 1900 behind the Callow Hotel in Big Pine are, from left to right, (seated) Ed Ober, Peachey Ober, their son Austin, Porte Jack, and Mattie ?; (standing) hotel owners Mrs. Callow and Tom Callow, Bridget ?, and "the cook." Jim Butler, who discovered the 1900 Tonopah silver strikes, bought the business in 1904 and renamed it the Butler Hotel. Little is known about the staff; the cook was Chinese, and Porte Jack and Mattie were Paiute. Like much of the early West, the Owens Valley was home to a diverse mix of immigrant and ethnic groups. Two-thirds of miners were noncitizens or foreign-born, mainly from Mexico and Chile. Farmers, cattlemen, and sheepmen often had roots in Ireland, France, Italy, Ireland, or England. The valley's Jewish families owned prominent mercantile businesses, and German immigrants operated many of the dozens of breweries in valley towns. At the bottom of the social ladder, Chinese worked as railroad and mining laborers, cooks, or laundry workers. (J.D. Black Papers, William H. Hannon Library, Loyola Marymount University.)

Bishop Creek looked like any other frontier town, but a high concentration of women, children, and churches gave it a more sedate feel. Other valley residents often called it "Gospel Swamp" for its water-saturated lowlands during spring runoff. Starting in 1864, the town prospered from agricultural trade with mining camps from Bodie to Panamint. This 1911 view looks south on Main Street, after the town incorporated and was renamed Bishop in 1903.

In 1886, Bishop residents, concerned that education in valley schools ended after grammar school, formed the Inyo Academy, the Owens Valley's first institution of higher learning. Eight teachers, including author Mary Austin, taught traditional high school subjects, plus Latin, Greek, music, and other offerings. The public Bishop High School replaced the financially troubled academy in 1902 and took over its imposing building. The high school's first graduating class is seen here on the steps that year.

The Nevada Power, Mining, and Milling Company (later the Nevada-California Power Company) built the first of five powerhouses in the Bishop Creek Hydroelectric complex in 1905. Above, Bishop teamsters Charles Collins and Walter Young (on horses) haul part of the second unit for Plant Four from the narrow gauge station at Laws. The plants produced electricity for local use, but most went to Nevada via long-distance transmission lines. For decades, large operating crews and their families lived in the plants' housing. Isolated by poor roads until 1966, they formed a unique company community in Bishop Creek Canyon. Southern California Edison operates the system today; employees live in the restored historic cottages at Plant Four. Below, this livery stable was one of two in Bishop in 1900. Essential fixtures in early towns, many were converted to garages as automobile use grew. (Above, Laws Museum and Historic Site.)

Above, a stagecoach stops in front of the Cosmopolitan Restaurant in Darwin in about 1900. Until 1910, when Southern Pacific completed the rail link from Mojave to the Owens Valley, stagecoach service provided the only passenger transportation between Southern California and the Owens Valley. Stagecoach drivers and teamsters hauling freight and Cerro Gordo bullion could rest and change teams at way stations, located at regular intervals between the valley and Los Angeles. The Olancha station, below, operated by rancher William Walker from his home at the southwest end of Owens Lake, functioned as the hub of business and social life in early Olancha. From 1871 to 1912, it was also the post office. The building is seen here in 1910, when Walker's son Web (second from left) was postmaster.

Originating in Mound House, Nevada, the narrow gauge Carson & Colorado Railroad was routed down the Owens Valley's eastern side to serve mining interests in the White-Inyo Mountains. By the time tracks were laid to Hawley (later Keeler), on Owens Lake's northeast side, in 1883, the mining boom had all but ended, and owners halted planned construction to Mojave. Despite its location far from valley towns, the line opened the isolated region to commerce and travel and spurred development of soda ash production and other mining operations near Owens Lake. The train is seen above in 1888 at Laws, the station for Bishop Creek. Below, Capt. Julius Keeler's namesake 42-block town at Owens Lake became a lively shipping and transportation hub, where train passengers continuing south boarded the twice-weekly Keeler stage for the 22-hour journey to Mojave.

For more than 70 years, a plume of black smoke and a sharp whistle signaled the approach of the narrow gauge "Slim Princess." It was, noted news reporter John Spears, "a passenger train, freight train, and milk train . . . but in order to economize, one engine is made to pull all three." Southern Pacific bought the struggling Carson & Colorado line in 1900, and as the Tonopah silver camps suddenly boomed, it soon recouped its investment. In later years, the trains kept a casual schedule, giving a lift to anyone walking the tracks and filling water barrels for prospectors. Stations several miles distant from the towns they served were often little more than lonely boxcar sidings, but most housed workers and became lively towns in their own right, with tidy homes, lawns, and gardens. At Kearsarge Station, earlier called Citrus, a colorful community of employees and their families lived across the tracks from the depot, and children from the large Gracey and Graziani families traveled five miles by wagon to and from school in Independence each day.

Three
WATER SEEKERS

A crowd of several hundred people watches water from the Los Angeles Aqueduct flow down the Alabama Spillway near Lone Pine after Owens Valley resistance leaders seized the aqueduct on November 16, 1924. The peaceful four-day "Picnic at the Alabama Gates" drew nationwide attention to the resisters' demands for reparations following Los Angeles' buyout of valley farms. (J.D. Black Papers, William H. Hannon Library, Loyola Marymount University.)

Seen above in this 1906 *Los Angeles Times* photograph are, from left to right, United States Reclamation Service engineer Joseph B. Lippincott, former Los Angeles mayor Fred Eaton, and Los Angeles Water Department chief engineer William Mulholland. Eaton had long envisioned bringing Owens River water south to ensure the city's future growth, and he urged Mulholland to design an aqueduct from the Owens Valley. Intending to profit from a joint private-municipal aqueduct, Eaton quietly began buying land along the river. Lippincott was also a consultant to Los Angeles and expressed support for a municipal project over an Owens Valley Reclamation reservoir then under study. The Reclamation Service deferred to the city's interest in the Owens River's water, and in July 1905, Los Angeles stunned Owens Valley residents with the announcement. Below, surveyors work in 1906 along the Owens River near Independence. (Above, Los Angeles Department of Water and Power.)

Los Angeles surveyors worked from a camp near Independence (above) starting in 1906. The previous September, Los Angeles voters had approved an initial aqueduct bond of $1.5 million. Arguing for its passage, water superintendent William Mulholland cited the city's commitment to growth: "If Los Angeles doesn't get this water, she won't need it." (Bruce Branson collection.)

Preliminary work along the aqueduct route began nearly two years before the start of construction in October 1908. Men using mules and scrapers, seen here near Owens Lake, built 500 miles of roads and trails through the desert, while Southern Pacific constructed a standard gauge supply link from Mojave into the Owens Valley. Workers installed hundreds of miles of telephone and transmission line and a temporary water pipeline along the 233-mile route.

In Los Angeles, support for the aqueduct was not unanimous. Mayor Fred Eaton escorted city officials through the Owens Valley in late 1905 to persuade those still skeptical of the project of its feasibility and future importance. They are seen above in Big Pine on November 13, 1905, with Eaton fourth from the left. The visitors later spoke of Los Angeles' "enviable position" in "having the control of such a magnificent water supply." Los Angeles appointed an independent board of highly-regarded engineers from around the nation to evaluate Mulholland's aqueduct plans. Together with Mulholland and other officials, they toured the aqueduct route in late 1906. Part of the group is seen below near Lone Pine. The consultants later reported, "We find the project admirable in conception and outline." (Above, Mulholland Album, Los Angeles Department of Water and Power.)

Aqueduct construction could not go forward without electric power. In July 1908, Los Angeles put a small 120-kilowatt hydroelectric plant into operation at Division Creek, near Big Pine. A 900-kilowatt turbine (above) at Cottonwood Creek Plant, south of Lone Pine, began generating electricity in November 1908. Together, the plants powered construction camps and machinery, including electric dipper dredgers (below) used for excavating the aqueduct's unlined canal north of the Alabama Hills. The Cottonwood turbine also supplied power to the city's cement plant near Tehachapi and later produced electricity for Owens Valley residents. An earlier version of the dredger, christened "Big Bill" by workers in honor of Mulholland, was used to dig the first several miles of canal south of the intake. Aqueduct worker Russell Spainhower (seen here atop the shaft), was later a Lone Pine rancher and civic leader.

Aqueduct workers gather at the Olancha camp mess house about 1909. With hiring under way by 1908, hundreds of workers headed to Los Angeles and Mojave to find work on the huge project. Many were recent immigrants—Greeks, Serbs, Swiss, Bulgarians, and Mexicans—or the hard-drinking, pick-and-shovel men known as "blanket stiffs." Most laborers averaged two weeks on

In all, 2,300 structures were used at the 57 camps and construction sites, including 50 powder magazines and 8 hospitals. Many could be dismantled and moved to a new location, as seen here near Lone Pine.

the job, collecting enough pay for a binge in Mojave's saloons before moving on to a new camp. For the rest, a job done well brought bonuses and pay increases. All were provided medical care. Mid-level clerical and engineering jobs often went to young men just out of college, eager to gain experience on "Mulholland's ditch." At one time, nearly 5,000 men worked on the aqueduct.

Most workers slept in tents or bunkhouses, but small frame homes and tent-houses were available to married men, and children could attend one-room schools in some camps. Cottonwood Power plant operator Walter Harris and his family lived in this tent starting in 1908.

A steam shovel excavates the aqueduct in what will be open lined canal between the north end of the Alabama Hills and Haiwee Reservoir. Dug entirely by power shovels, this section was considered comparatively easy work, despite the giant boulders that slowed progress. The shovels continued to prove their worth in the progressively harsher terrain farther south. (Los Angeles Department of Water and Power.)

Following close behind the excavation, crews lined the canal using concrete made with "good, clean gravel" from the ancient beach line of nearby Owens Lake. The plaster for the six-foot side sections used tufa cement from Haiwee. The cost per foot, in direct charges, of the 37 miles of lined conduit section was $8.38. (Los Angeles Department of Water and Power.)

At 233 miles long, the aqueduct as completed in 1913 was hailed as an engineering marvel. It included 3 reservoirs, 12 miles of steel siphon, 43 miles of tunnels, and 98 miles of covered conduit. The first 60 miles of aqueduct to Haiwee Reservoir was open canal. To maintain the gradual fall that permitted the aqueduct's all-gravity flow, it was then routed through increasingly rugged terrain that presented formidable engineering and construction challenges. Shown here, the steel pressure siphon completed in March 1913 across desolate Jawbone Canyon north of Mojave was considered, according to the 1916 *Construction of the Los Angeles Aqueduct Final Report*, "the most noteworthy pipe in the United States." Manufactured at an East Coast mill in sections weighing up to 26 tons, the pipe arrived by train at Cinco, north of Mojave, and from there traveled to Jawbone Canyon on specially built wagons pulled by 52-mule teams. The Jawbone construction camp is visible at right. (Los Angeles Department of Water and Power.)

Los Angeles officials and Owens Valley engineers watch as Owens River water flows through the intake north of Independence on February 13, 1913. Moments before, William Mulholland had opened the gates that released the water on its first official journey south to Los Angeles, as Bessie Van Norman (left) the wife of Owens Valley division chief H.A. Van Norman, cracked a ceremonial champagne bottle on the structure's north side. The concrete inscription there reads "Los Angeles Aqueduct Intake, MCMXI." Completed in 1911, the intake remains in use today. (Above, Los Angeles Department of Water and Power.)

Above, at the aqueduct's southern terminus in September 1913, William Mulholland (right) watches testing of the spillway into San Fernando Reservoir that he dubbed the "Cascade." Soon after, he set off on a final inspection of the aqueduct prior to the formal opening, scheduled for November 5. That day, more than 30,000 people arrived by buggy, horseback, automobile, and train to witness the long-awaited Owens River water gush down the Cascade (right). Many brought cups for a first drink of the water that was now theirs. Preceding Mulholland's famously terse speech: "There it is, take it," was soprano Ellen Beach Yaw's rendition of "Hail the Water," when she sang, "Lift your voice in gratitude, a river now is here . . . For God has brought us waters pure, that Eden we regain."

Despite unresolved differences with Los Angeles over future water allocations, Owens Valley residents settled into an uneasy coexistence with the city in the years after the aqueduct opened. As farm prices rose nationwide and heavy Sierra winters ensured sufficient water for both valley farmers and the surplus available to Los Angeles, land agents and business owners promoted a mood of hopeful optimism. "Inyo County is just awakening to its limitless possibilities," a 1917 report proclaims. Near Independence, irrigation developer George Chaffey's Owens Valley Improvement Company subdivided 1,200 acres of former ranchland, advertised the irrigated parcels nationwide, and in 1912, planted 20,000 apple trees. Buyers could also purchase lots in the subdivision's new town of Manzanar, Spanish for "apple orchard." Below, Indian laborers are at work haying in Round Valley about 1920.

Agricultural values and output climbed and peaked after 1910. Dairies and livestock production flourished, and fruit growers envisioned an Owens Valley apple industry comparable to that in Washington State. In good harvest years, orchards at Red Mountain Ranch (below), as well as those at Manzanar and Bishop, produced tons of prizewinning apples, including these displayed (right) at the California State Fair. Pears seemed promising as well; growers planted 20,000 pear trees in 1921 alone. The 1910 Southern Pacific rail link to Los Angeles opened long-inaccessible Southern California markets to Owens Valley farmers, and together with improved roads, brought increased commerce into the valley. By the early 1920s, however, the newfound optimism had dimmed, as drought spread over much of the Southwest, Owens Valley farmers felt the effects of a nationwide decline in agricultural prices, and Los Angeles' astounding growth brought demands for more water.

Local women watch as water flows under pressure from a well east of Independence, the first drilled by Los Angeles starting in 1910. The city drilled dozens of new wells after 1917, as dry conditions increased the valley's agricultural water consumption and reduced the surplus water available to Los Angeles.

By 1927, Los Angeles was operating 150 wells with depths of up to 850 feet. Here, a well near Big Pine discharges groundwater into a canal. As pumping lowered the valley's groundwater levels and adversely affected water rights and agriculture adjacent to the wells, farmers obtained court injunctions to halt the pumping. (J.D. Black Papers, William H. Hannon Library, Loyola Marymount University.)

In 1922, facing exponential growth and new water shortages, Los Angeles began buying water rights north of the intake and moved to control the valley's irrigation canals. Many owners gladly sold, while others joined sellers' pools to demand higher prices or refused to sell altogether. As town businesses suffered and property values plummeted, resistance leaders demanded compensation and the buyout of nonagricultural properties. The seizure of the aqueduct at the Alabama Spillway on November 16, 1924, (above) attracted the attention of state officials, celebrities, and a sympathetic national press, but won from Los Angeles only a promise of more negotiations. Below, Los Angeles officials inspect an irrigation ditch near Bishop in the early 1930s. By then, the city owned 95 percent of the agricultural land and water rights in the Owens Valley. (Above, author's collection; below, Los Angeles Department of Water and Power.)

Negotiations over reparations, property price-setting, and town buyouts dragged on and repeatedly broke down through the late 1920s. On May 27, 1927, Owens Valley resisters dynamited the aqueduct's No Name Siphon south of Little Lake (above). It was the most powerful of 10 aqueduct blasts within a six-week period, and it again focused national attention on the "Owens Valley Water Wars." Organized opposition ended suddenly that August, however, when auditors closed the Inyo County Bank branches owned by Bishop resistance leaders Mark Watterson (below, second from left) and his brother Wilfred (second from right) after the discovery of $800,000 in missing funds. Much of it was the life savings of Owens Valley residents who had deposited payments they had received from Los Angeles for their properties. The Wattersons were convicted of embezzlement and sent to prison at San Quentin. (Below, Laws Museum and Historic Site.)

Few orchards were still producing when this photograph was taken looking north at the Manzanar fruit-growing subdivision in the early 1930s. Independence is in the distance, and the aqueduct curves from the north on the right. After buying out the entire subdivision, Los Angeles continued to grow and harvest fruit at Manzanar into the early 1930s, shipping it out under a City of Los Angeles label. With most agricultural land in city ownership, abandoned farm homes and fields, mainly in the northern valley, marked the former properties of owners who had left, including the farmers below, or had given up agriculture altogether. Others who sold remained on their former land as tenants and continued to farm, but without a guarantee of water. (Above, the Benjamin and Gladys Thomas Air Photo Archives, UCLA.)

An early-1940s map illustrates the Los Angeles Aqueduct system after completion in 1941 of the Mono Basin Project and the Long Valley Dam and Reservoir, named Crowley Lake in memory of Owens Valley priest and civic leader John J. Crowley. Some historians have suggested that earlier construction of the dam to regulate and store the Owens River's flow could have prevented the drawn-out 1920s "water wars." Others argue that given Los Angeles' unprecedented growth, it would have only postponed the city's eventual acquisition of nearly all Owens Valley land and water rights. In the years after the resistance movement collapsed in 1927, Los Angeles and the Owens Valley renewed efforts to find common ground on the sale of remaining property. In 1929, Los Angeles announced it would buy all land still under private ownership, if owners wished to sell. Many town properties would be leased back. By 1938, Los Angeles owned 85 percent of land in the Owens Valley's towns. (Los Angeles Department of Water and Power.)

Four

INTO A NEW ERA

Automobiles line Bishop's busy main street in 1946. By 1930, Inyo County had lost almost 10 percent of its population, with Bishop hit the hardest. The town and the valley gradually rebounded through the next two decades, as residents worked to build a new tourist and recreation economy, and Los Angeles sold many town properties back into private ownership.

With the goal of charting a new economic course for the Owens Valley, the 30-member Inyo Associates, a leadership group formed in 1935 by Lone Pine priest John J. Crowley and businessman Ralph Merritt, called on Los Angeles to work cooperatively by promoting tourism, opening city-owned lands for recreation, and returning town properties to private ownership. Above, Crowley (center, in black) is in costume for the Wedding of the Waters pageant he organized to celebrate the completion of the highway between Death Valley and Whitney Portal in 1937. The three-day event generated nationwide publicity for the valley, as historic modes of transportation, from Indian runner to airplane, carried water more than 100 miles from the nation's highest lake near Mount Whitney to Badwater in Death Valley, the lowest point in North America. Below, a 20-mule-team wagon transports the water east from Lone Pine.

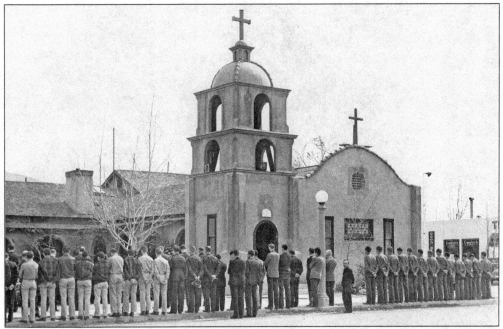

The death of the beloved "Padre," John J. Crowley, in a road accident on March 17, 1940, at age 48 stunned the Eastern Sierra. Nearly 1,000 people, including Los Angeles civic and water officials, attended the funeral, held at the small Santa Rosa Church in Lone Pine. A Death Valley Civilian Conservation Corps unit stood guard, honoring the Irish-born priest revered by many and called by the *Inyo Independent* "a great man among men." (Maturango Museum.)

Los Angeles Department of Water and Power employees are seen here at the Owens Valley headquarters in Independence. Built in 1928, the complex included warehouses and maintenance shops. Many employees were local residents who had joined the city's workforce after losing other livelihoods. With a dozen or more city-built homes available to workers, and others rented or owned by Los Angeles or Inyo County employees, Independence resembled a city-county "company town."

The disappearance of farms and ranches left nearly two-thirds of Indian workers without livelihoods. By the 1930s, many lived in desperate conditions on Los Angeles–owned land near towns. Through the 1937 Owens Valley Land Exchange, the federal government traded nearly 3,000 acres of allotted Indian land for 1,400 acres of Los Angeles land to be used for new reservations at Bishop, Big Pine, and Lone Pine. Above, from left to right, Daisy Williams, Rosie Piper, and Sally Jackson listen to speeches at the Land Exchange barbecue in Bishop. Below, near Big Pine, a Los Angeles official stands in an alfalfa field on land leased to William Hines. Early lessees did not have a guarantee of irrigation water; many soon shifted to raising stock. (Below, Los Angeles Department of Water Power.)

Los Angeles Department of Water and Power (LADWP) hydrographers Dave McCoy (left) and Claude James measure the Eastern Sierra snowpack in 1947. McCoy reads scales showing the water content of a snow core in the attached metal tube. Each winter and spring, hydrographers skied into snow courses from Cottonwood Lakes to the Mammoth Lakes Basin, some of which had been in use since measuring began in 1926. Data from the surveys enabled engineers to forecast runoff and plan water exports. McCoy started work with the city in 1937 and became a hydrographer in 1941. On weekends, he pursued his passion for skiing by running rope tows at McGee Creek and Mammoth, organizing ski races, and coaching young racers. His hydrographer's knowledge and skiing experience convinced him that conditions for ski development were ideal on Mammoth Mountain's north side. With a 25-year permit from the United States Forest Service, he left the LADWP in 1953 and, over the next half-century, turned Mammoth Mountain into a world-class ski destination. (Los Angeles Department of Water and Power.)

In 1953, Los Angeles completed three hydroelectric plants in the 10-mile-long Owens River Gorge, a deep gash in the volcanic tuff north of Bishop. In this view looking south, the Middle Gorge plant is at the bottom. With the river diverted for power production, the gorge remained dry until 1991, when the city began mandated re-watering to restore riparian habitat and sport fishing. (Library of Congress, Historic American Engineering Record.)

The Second Los Angeles Aqueduct, or "second barrel," completed in 1970, increased Eastern Sierra water delivery capacity by nearly 50 percent. The 155-mile-long, mostly covered pipeline roughly parallels the first aqueduct from Haiwee Reservoir south. In 1972, citing environmental damage due to increased groundwater pumping to fill the aqueducts, Inyo County sued Los Angeles for noncompliance with the recently enacted California Environmental Quality Act. (Los Angeles Department of Water and Power.)

Acceptance by both sides of the Inyo-LA Long Term Water Agreement followed 19 years of legal challenges and protracted negotiations. A controversial and complex compromise, it calls for, among other requirements, joint county-city management of Los Angeles' groundwater pumping levels. Here, Los Angeles mayor Tom Bradley (left) and Inyo County supervisor Keith Bright sign the agreement in 1991, as Inyo County Water Department counsel Greg James looks on.

The Owens River winds downstream in this recent photograph looking southeast along the Inyo Mountains. At the lower center, most of the river's flow is diverted into the Los Angeles Aqueduct, on the right. Since Los Angeles began court-mandated re-watering of the Lower Owens River (LOR) below the intake in 2006, wildlife and vegetation absent for 90 years have reappeared. The white areas are alkaline deposits. (Author's collection.)

Hollywood moviemakers discovered Lone Pine's stunning location possibilities in 1920 when they filmed the silent western *The Round-Up* starring Fatty Arbuckle entirely in the Alabama Hills. Since then, the town has hosted crews for nearly 400 feature films. Silent star Buck Jones, who made several B westerns in the area, is seen here with costar Barbara Bennett during the filming of *Black Jack* in the Alabama Hills in 1927. (Author's collection.)

Republic Pictures' 1938 *Under Western Stars* marked Roy Rogers's starring debut. He is on horseback, at right, during filming in the Alabama Hills. Rogers returned often to make his popular "singing cowboy" movies. The same year, the 10-week shoot of the classic *Gunga Din* brought Cary Grant and other stars to Lone Pine, together with four elephants and a crew of several hundred that re-created 19th-century India in the Alabama Hills.

Movie crews enjoyed filming in Lone Pine, and residents took the presence of stars and crews in stride. Many worked on the productions as cowboys and extras. Above, cast members of the 1957 film *The Lonely Man* showed their appreciation by planting a new "lone pine" to replace the town's original 1860s namesake tree. Seen here are local Bureau of Land Management personnel and Boy Scouts, together with Inyo County supervisor John Lubken standing at the left of the sign. On the right of the sign, from left to right, are actor Jack Palance, actress Eileen Aiken, director Henry Levin, and actor Anthony Perkins. Below, frequent visitor Gregory Peck returned to Lone Pine in 1962 with Debbie Reynolds, Robert Mitchum, and others to shoot scenes for *How the West Was Won,* including this big Indian-attack sequence. (Above, Chris Langley Collection; below, Lone Pine Museum of Film History.)

Pres. Franklin Roosevelt implemented the Civilian Pilot Training Program in 1938 to create a large pool of future military pilots. Throughout World War II, the program offered ground school and flight training to thousands of college students and eventually trained nearly 450,000 pilots at 1,500

Military personnel from Big Pine, some only recently returned from the Pacific and Europe, have gathered on Main Street for this photograph after the 1946 Memorial Day parade.

flight schools nationwide, including those at Lone Pine, Manzanar/Inyo County, Independence, and Bishop Airports. Cadets and trainers of the Independence Primary Civilian Pilot Training class, September-December, 1942, are seen here in front of their Boeing Stearman.

A Nisei soldier, one of 174 draftees and volunteers from Manzanar War Relocation Center, visits his parents in 1944. Most served in the 442nd Regimental Combat Team, 100th Infantry Battalion, a highly-decorated all-Nisei unit that fought in North Africa and Europe. (Toyo Miyatake photograph, Toyo Miyatake Studio.)

Located south of Independence, Manzanar War Relocation Center was the first of 10 barbed-wire-enclosed "camps" nationwide hastily built to confine nearly 120,000 persons of Japanese ancestry removed from the West Coast during World War II. Opened in March 1942, the mile-square Manzanar center housed more than 10,000 people. Most were from Southern California; two-thirds were American-born. Over nearly four years, internees transformed the dusty, windblown site and its hundreds of flimsy barracks into a habitable community, creating gardens and parks, setting up churches, social clubs, and sports leagues, and staffing mess halls, schools, a hospital, and libraries. Above, a woman tends a victory garden, one of several in the camp's firebreaks. Below, internees wait in line for meals at one of the 36 mess halls. (Both, War Relocation Authority Photographs by Dorothea Lange, National Archives NWDNS-210-G-C677 and C671.)

Attempts to commercially harvest the pure salt found in the remote Saline Valley, east of the Inyo Mountains, had long been hampered by the difficulty of transporting it. In 1911, the Saline Valley Salt Company began construction on a 13.5-mile electric tram designed to transport salt up 7,600 feet from Saline Valley, over the Inyo crest, and down 5,100 feet to a mill and rail terminal at Tramway, near Keeler. Here, Tramway workers welcome the arrival of the first salt carrier on July 2, 1913. In its first months of operation, the company shipped up to 15 railcars of salt each week, but even that large volume could not offset the tram's high building and operating costs. After passing through several owners, it closed down for the last time in 1933.

Dolomite's "mountain of marble" near Keeler contained superior-quality white, variegated, and yellow dolomitic marble. Inyo Marble Company began quarrying it in 1885. In 1890, it sent 200 railcars of Inyo marble to San Francisco for use in the Mills Building, then the tallest building in the West. Marble works foreman Al Staudinger is on the right in this early-1900s photograph. (J.D. Black Papers, William H. Hannon Library, Loyola Marymount University.)

In 1923, Detroit-based Champion Sillimanite Inc. located a large deposit of high-grade andalusite, used in the manufacture of spark plugs, on the steep western flank of the White Mountains north of Bishop. Inaccessible by road, the Champion "Sparkplug" mine depended on mules for transporting equipment and supplies up to the mine and bringing the ore down 3,000 feet for transfer to the railroad. The mine operated until 1945. (Laws Museum and Historic Site.)

Inyo Development Company's soda-processing plant at Keeler, opened in 1887, was the first of four Owens Lake installations that over nearly 80 years produced millions of tons of soda ash, used mainly in manufacturing glass and cleaning compounds. Above, workers harvest crude soda, or trona, deposited by the evaporation of lake brine in huge solar ponds. Natural Soda Products, started in 1912 by Bishop's Watterson brothers, introduced more efficient production methods at its plant south of Keeler, seen below in the 1920s. These plants, together with installations at Cartago and Bartlett, on Owens Lake's west side, employed hundreds of workers, many of them from southern Inyo's large Mexican community, who lived with their families in company-built towns near the plants. After World War I, fluctuating demand and water diversions forced revised processing methods and frequent plant closures.

As agriculture declined, Southern Pacific relied on transporting borax, soda ash, talc, ore products, and livestock to keep its Owens Valley lines viable. Above, at Owenyo, narrow gauge trains from the north interchanged with the standard gauge line from Mojave, built in 1910 to supply the construction of the Los Angeles Aqueduct. The station is seen looking north from the high line trestle used to transfer bulk ore and other products from the narrow to standard-width cars. Workers moved sacked soda ash and other freight across the docks in the center and used a hand-operated gantry crane for larger transfers. The standard gauge train turned on a "Y" track to return south. Below, enjoying lunch in a caboose in 1947, are, from left to right, two unidentified men, John Shepherd, longtime narrow gauge engineer Walter Ferguson, and conductor Jim Brennan.

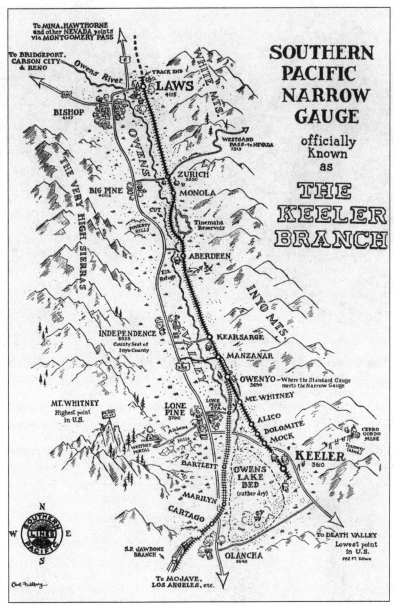

Soon after acquiring the Carson & Colorado Railroad in 1900, Southern Pacific began converting many of the line's Nevada segments to standard gauge, but "Slim Princess" steam locomotives continued scheduled runs on the 71.33-mile narrow-gauge Keeler Branch between Laws and Keeler until 1954. The line was a commercial and travel lifeline for the isolated valley for nearly 80 years. The addition of the 1910 standard gauge "Jawbone" extension from Mojave gave the Owens Valley direct rail connections to Southern California for the first time. In the following decades, the two lines carried mail and passengers, and, despite the costly transfers at Owenyo, hauled out much of the valley's diminishing agricultural production, even as it brought in equipment, goods, and supplies for the growing number of hotels, stores, restaurants, and gas stations. As highways improved and automobile and truck use increased through the 1920s and 1930s, rail traffic declined. Southern Pacific began reductions in scheduled freight and passenger service starting in 1932. (John Hungerford, author's collection.)

Above, bidding farewell to an era, 300 railfans ride along as Engine No. 9, the last of the "Slim Princess" steam locomotives, makes its final official run from Owenyo to Keeler on October 16, 1954. Replaced by a narrow gauge diesel engine, No. 9 stayed on standby status until April 29, 1960, when Southern Pacific terminated the narrow gauge line between Keeler and Laws and began removing tracks. That date marked the end of the last remaining narrow gauge common carrier west of the Rockies—and one of the most profitable. Southern Pacific transferred Engine No. 9, seen below on the gallows turntable at Laws, in a gift deed to the City of Bishop and Inyo County, along with cars, equipment, and the Laws Station. (Below, Curtis Phillips, Laws Museum.)

Five
VACATIONLAND

Pomona photographer Burton Frasher's widely circulated postcards of the 1920s and 1930s boosted tourism in the Eastern Sierra. In this one, Mount Whitney, the highest peak in the contiguous United States, beckons to the adventurous: "Off for the top of the U.S.A." Lone Pine resident Gus Marsh engineered the first pack trail up the 14,497-foot peak in 1904 and supervised construction of the Smithsonian Institution Shelter at the summit. (Author's collection.)

Sawmill operator Col. Sherman Stevens was reportedly the first to transplant golden trout into the Eastern Sierra when he carried 13 of the prized fish in a coffee can from the Western Sierra Kern River drainage to easterly-flowing Cottonwood Creek in 1876. Today, golden trout are found mainly in the Eastern Sierra's high-elevation backcountry lakes. After 1900, fisheries experts established hatchery-raised rainbow, eastern brook, and brown trout in the Owens River and many of its tributary streams and lakes. In the 1890s, judge George Hall led trout-fishing development in the Big Pine Creek drainage, where the women above show off their catches in about 1900. Below, with travel trailers and tents, anglers in the 1950s could enjoy home comforts on Eastern Sierra fishing trips. (Above, J.D. Black Papers, William H. Hannon Library, Loyola Marymount University; below, Los Angeles Department of Water and Power.)

By 1915, transporting fish from distant hatcheries to local waterways was becoming more costly. That year, California Fish and Game officials chose a 40-acre site on Oak Creek, near Independence, for an Owens Valley hatchery. Local residents bought the land from pioneer Andrew Bell and deeded it to the state, and Fish and Game Commissioner M.J. Connell called for a building that would "match the mountains and last forever." Workers fitted together 3,500 tons of local granite rocks to form the structure's two-foot-thick walls. Completed in 1917 and seen above in the late 1920s, the majestic Mount Whitney Hatchery was the world's largest fish-rearing facility. Below, golden trout eggs collected from the Cottonwood Lakes, together with millions of eggs produced annually at the hatchery from rainbow, eastern, and brown trout brood stock, were kept in incubators. Newly hatched fish and fingerlings matured in troughs inside the hatchery.

Beginning in the late 1920s, promotional materials that had once touted the region's farming opportunities were instead extolling its scenic wonders and well-stocked fishing streams. In the following decades, widespread advertising increasingly drove the development of Eastern Sierra tourism. The Los Angeles Department of Water and Power produced much of it, including this 1940s brochure. Its imagery of an Owens Valley "Vacationland" was geared mainly to Southern California urban dwellers, whose post–World War II prosperity, better automobiles, and shorter workweeks made recreation-oriented escapes possible. By the 1960s, tourists accounted for 80 percent of traffic through the Owens Valley. Today, this once isolated land welcomes millions of visitors from around the world. (Los Angeles Department of Water and Power.)

The Owens Valley's "head booster," Father John J. Crowley, used every opportunity to publicize the area's recreational wonders. When the first day of fishing season fell on a Sunday in 1938, he scheduled a "Fisherman's Mass" at 3:30 a.m. at his Lone Pine church to allow Catholics to attend mass and still compete for hungry trout in the early-morning hours. Parishioners and visitors, he said, could come dressed for fishing; rods and reels would receive a blessing. Above, Father Crowley blesses Catherine Byrne's tackle as Bishop teacher Aim Morhardt waits his turn in a photograph taken by Bishop photographer Curtis Phillips. Crowley invited Phillips to the mass, and his photographs accompanied features in *Westways* travel magazine. Below, from left to right, Owens Valley residents Wayne, Lucille, and Gwen Calloway display their catch on a camping trip at Monache Meadows in about 1936.

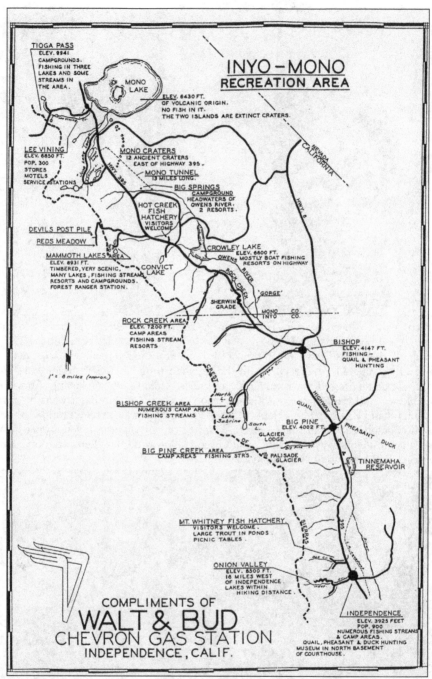

This recreation map of the northern Owens Valley and Mono County, drawn by Owens Valley artist Jack Fair about 1950, was posted at Walt and Bud's Chevron station on Highway 395 in Independence. Early efforts to promote tourism were often hampered by the lack of road access to the Eastern Sierra's scenic wonders. Before 1930, most secondary roads were little more than widened, rocky trails. Federal, state, and local agencies, together with the City of Los Angeles, worked to grade roads, build trails and campgrounds, and improve access to popular fishing and camping areas. (Map by Jack Fair, author's collection.)

Members of the High Sierra Recreation Association have gathered for this publicity photograph at Palisade Glacier in about 1934. The group formed in 1929 to promote tourism and "the general development of the entire area" through organized advertising. Lending support and resources was an honorary committee of local and statewide civic and business dignitaries headed by Bishop native and National Park Service director Horace Albright.

Seen here in 1928, R.J. Bandhauer's general store in Independence advertised itself as a one-stop tourist headquarters, with maps, food, camping supplies, and fishing tackle available to vacationers. Bandhauer was a founding member of Inyo Associates, an organization of civic and business leaders formed in 1935 to enlist the help of Los Angeles in developing Eastern Sierra recreation and tourism. (Author's collection.)

To introduce visitors to the Eastern Sierra and showcase the recreational uses of its land, the City of Los Angeles, together with valley agencies and businesses, mounted exhibits at fairs and travel shows. The display above, at the 1954 Los Angeles Sportsmen's Vacation, Boat, and Trailer Show, features a mountain cabin, together with a waterfall and a trout-filled aquarium. Representing the High Sierra Packers Association, formed in 1934, Lone Pine packers Frank Chrysler and Ted Cook drew enthusiastic crowds when they brought pack animals to the city and set up camp outside the exhibit hall. Below, a pack train and riders head out from Parcher's Camp in Bishop Creek Canyon, about 1935. More than 40 pack outfits once operated in Inyo and Mono Counties, but over time, backcountry restrictions and high costs have reduced that number by more than half. (Above, Los Angeles Department of Water and Power.)

As skiers discovered Mammoth Mountain in the 1930s, Owens Valley residents were starting up modest ski operations on their own nearby slopes. Enterprising Independence friends, including ski pioneer Dave McCoy, used a Ford Model A truck to run an early rope tow at the saddle above nearby Seven Pines. By 1941, with tows operating at Whitney Portal and Big Pine Canyon, Independence mechanic O.K. Kelley and hydrographer Vic Taylor built an 800-foot rope tow and a ski hut high in Onion Valley, attracting both local skiers and regulars from Southern California. Below, hunters display ducks from marshes and canals near Big Pine around 1930.

In the late 1940s, Southern California businessman John Grant attempted to establish the town of Grant on his property south of Olancha. Although denied a post office, the town did appear on signage and state highway maps. A motel, café, and gas station served travelers, and from Grant's airstrip nearby, the Airlift Pack Station flew fishermen into the Sierra backcountry. This advertisement appeared in a 1957 recreation guide.

Built in 1924 and owned by the Whorff family after 1925, Bishop's Kittie Lee Inn (pictured) was renowned for its comfort and hospitality and was a favorite with vacationers, dignitaries, and Hollywood celebrities. During World War II, pilots training at Bishop Airport used the dining room as a barracks; it later became the famous Copper Kettle Coffee Shop. Today, Whiskey Creek Restaurant occupies part of the site where the inn once stood.

Visitors load a tour bus outside the Winnedumah Hotel in Independence in February 1928. Businessman Walter Dow built the hotel in 1927, and Fred and Hattie Schaefer later owned it. For more than 70 years, it welcomed vacationers, moviemakers, and officials on business at the county courthouse. A brass plaque in the cavernous wood-paneled lobby recounted the Paiute legend of "Winnedumah," which means, "Stay right where you are." (Author's collection.)

By the mid-1920s, large movie companies were arriving regularly in Lone Pine to film in the Alabama Hills. The town lacked modern lodging facilities until 1923, when Lone Pine Lumber Company owner Walter Dow built the Dow Hotel, seen here in a 1933 advertisement. Now expanded and called the Dow Villa, the hotel remains a headquarters for tourism and moviemaking in southern Inyo County. (Author's collection.)

Nestled high in scenic Big Pine Canyon, Glacier Lodge was one of several rustic resorts built in the early 1900s near alpine lakes and fishing streams in the Eastern Sierra. Started in 1917, it was sold in 1933, and the new owners expanded this magnificent lodge building, seen here in 1934. By then, a graded secondary road into Big Pine Canyon made the resort easily accessible from Los Angeles, and it became a haven for fishermen, families, and Hollywood actors. Behind it is the Palisade Glacier, a remnant of Ice Age glaciers that sculpted and polished the Sierra's granite canyons and created moraines, or vast boulder fields, as they advanced. Fire destroyed the main lodge three times, most recently in 1998, and only the outlying cabins remain. (Author's collection.)

Six

LOCAL LIFE

These bathing beauties at the Keeler Swimming Club drew an enthusiastic crowd in August 1929. Built by workers from the Natural Soda Products plant nearby, the pool had a bathhouse and a sandy beach. It stood at the edge of Owens Lake, near where Cerro Gordo silver bullion was once loaded on the steamer *Bessie Brady* for the trip across the lake to Cartago.

The student body and faculty advisors of Big Pine High School are seen here in front of the school in this 1939 photograph taken by Bishop photographer Curtis Phillips.

Hard at work in this 1927 Lone Pine High School typing class are, from left to right, Paul Diaz, Margaret Bagwell, Ivadell Wiltfang, Mary Skinner, Delphina Carrasco, and an unidentified girl. Many graduates of Owens Valley high schools have continued on to colleges and universities, usually in Southern California. Others have stayed to join family businesses or to take jobs with Inyo County and other government agencies.

At the Manzanar fruit-growing community, elementary-age children walked to the two-room schoolhouse, but high school students rode this bus, seen here in 1922, six miles to Owens Valley High School in Independence. Bus driver Mabel Wilder, a teacher at the high school, picked up students from ranches and farms throughout the area. "There were sometimes more students from Manzanar than Independence," former student Omie Mairs recalled. (Author's collection.)

Children from Olancha and Cartago stand in front of their one-room school about 1940. Built in Olancha on donated ranchland in 1917, it was used until a new multiroom school opened in 1949.

Owens Valley women attend a garden party hosted by Bessie Van Norman on June 30, 1912, at her Independence home. Van Norman (third row, far left) came to the Owens Valley from Los Angeles as a young bride in 1908. Her husband, engineer H.A. Van Norman, headed aqueduct construction in the Owens Valley Division.

Wong's Café in Lone Pine was popular in the 1920s, when this man, said to be its owner, sat for a portrait by Allen Ramsey. Known locally as Wong Coon or Wong Koong, he lived most of his life at Keeler. Chinese immigrants came to the Owens Valley in the late 1800s as mining and railroad laborers. By the early 1900s, many were working as cooks in local restaurants and a few owned businesses.

Photographer Allen Ramsey recorded the wedding of Concha Lozano and Charles Gonzalez on November 2, 1936, at the Santa Rosa Catholic Church in Lone Pine. Father John J. Crowley officiated, and many of southern Inyo's Mexican families attended. "It was a big wedding," the bride later recalled. The wedding party includes, from left to right, (sitting) Concha Lozano Gonzalez; (second row) Nell Martinez, unidentified, Charles Gonzalez, Lillian Munoz, and Rosie Cabo; (third row) Jasper Munoz, Lupe Lozano, Mathias Perez, and Mauro Martinez. Concha lived much of her childhood and adult life in company housing at the soda ash plants in Keeler, Cartago, and Bartlett, where most of the men in her family worked. Charles was employed at the Pacific Alkali soda ash plant at Bartlett. He and Connie lived there for many years and raised four children.

The Bishop Harvest Festival, started in 1911, replaced county fairs held since 1885 and borrowed from the Paiute Fandango that celebrated the annual pine-nut harvest. Featured attractions were Indian dancing and baby shows, and in 1912, an Alfalfa Palace built with 80 tons of baled hay. This lavish parade entry the same year was sponsored by the West Bishop School. Organizers discontinued the festival as farming declined in the 1920s.

Easter Sunrise services in the Sierra foothills are an Owens Valley tradition. With Mount Whitney as a backdrop, this 1932 service was held at what is now Lone Pine Campground. By the following year, Civilian Conservation Corps Camp 2921 was occupying the site. Housed in tents and later barracks, 200 young men excavated the Whitney Portal road and built trails and campgrounds.

The Fort Independence Indian Band, seen above in about 1915, performed at parades and events around the valley. White musicians in Independence provided instruments and taught early members to play. The band includes, from left to right, (sitting) Johnnie Symmes, Pete Thomas, Ben Hunter, Ed Lewis, and Jim Earl; (standing) Fred Glen, Tony Harris, Alex Patton, Jack Lang, Cleveland Buff, Harrison Diaz, and Jim Reynolds. Below, Independence Volunteer Fire Department trucks cool off spectators at the town's 2011 Fourth of July parade. July Fourth celebrations have been an Independence tradition since 1866, when the town was named for nearby Fort Independence. In the early 1900s, dancing at the famous Pavilion kicked off festivities the night before. The parade, barbecue, old-fashioned games, and fireworks finale are still part of the celebration. Past years have also featured historical pageants, parachute exhibitions, military flyovers, and bingo games. (Below, Michael Pietrobon photograph.)

FOURTH OF JULY
KEOUGH
RADIUM HOT SPRINGS

SUNDAY AFTERNOON, JULY THIRD

BIG Novelty Water Events

SPECIAL DIVING
: EXHIBITION :

Regular Sat. Nite
DANCE
JULY SECOND!

FREE For All Race Events

FOR MEN, WOMEN
: and CHILDREN :

Regular Sat. Nite
DANCE
JULY SECOND!

Monday Morning, July 4th	Monday Afternoon, July 4th
CHILDREN'S SUMMER FINALS JUNIOR OLYMPIC TRYOUTS	THIRTY ROUNDS OF FAST BOXING! Big THREE ROUND BATTLE ROYAL
Supervisor S. B. Nylander . . . Director	Local and Imported Talent . . . Ten Entrants

BIG EXHIBITION AERIAL FIREWORKS - NUMEROUS BEAUTIFUL SET PIECES

BIG FOURTH OF JULY DANCE!

DANCING 9 to 2 a. m.

Keough Six Piece Orchestra - - - - - - Admission $1.50

Keough's Hot Springs, originally known as Keough Radium Hot Springs, was the place to go in the 1920s and 1930s. Located south of Bishop, it was developed as a health and recreation resort by Bishop's Keough family and opened on August 7, 1919, with 1,000 Owens Valley residents on hand to swim in the new 100-foot spring-fed pool and dance the foxtrot in the open-air pavilion nearby. For centuries before that, the Paiute considered the three springs sacred and used them for healing and bathing. The water has remained a constant 127 degrees Fahrenheit since it was first measured in 1859. Today, it is fed into a spray system that cools it for the swimming pool. Fishermen's cabins and a campground accommodated tourists, but Keough's was above all a center of social life for the Owens Valley. Longtime residents recalled swimming in the children's and "grown-up" pools, dancing to live bands, and the diving competitions, boxing matches, and Easter egg hunts with hundreds of eggs. This full-page advertisement in the local newspaper promises a memorable Fourth of July celebration in 1932. (Author's collection.)

Keough's hosted end-of-year swim parties on staggered days for each Owens Valley school. Above, Big Pine Grammar School students have fun at their party in June 1933. Below, Christmas angels are ready for their school pageant on a chilly day at Owenyo Station in the 1920s. Much of Owenyo's town, including a restaurant and several homes, consisted of converted boxcars. Residents who grew up there have vivid recollections of the drafty boxcar school and its colorful teachers. (Below, Irma Cline collection.)

The Independence Senators Little League team (above) presents fresh Eastern Sierra trout to Los Angeles Dodgers manager Walter Alston (center) at the Los Angeles Coliseum on August 13, 1961. Organized by Independence businessman Omie Mairs and his wife, Glorian (far left), the Dodgers baseball trips became an annual event, with buses hired to take townspeople along. Starting in 1962, the Dodgers hosted "Independence Day" at their new stadium in Chavez Ravine, and Dodgers players who came to Independence to fish often helped coach the local teams. Below, Lone Pine High School teacher Vernon Raker instructs a physical education class in putting at the nine-hole Mount Whitney Golf Club in 1962. Local schools have traditionally incorporated skiing and other Eastern Sierra recreational activities into their sports programs. (Above, Glorian Mairs collection; below, Lone Pine High School photograph, author's collection.)

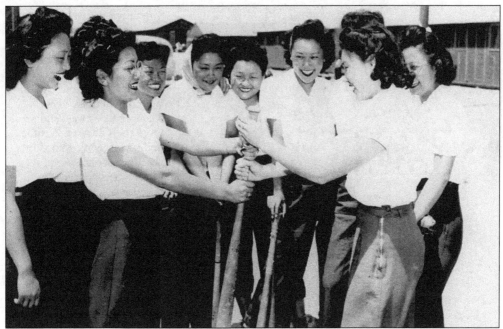

By the early summer of 1942, shouts of "play ball!" rang out across Manzanar War Relocation Center as 100 men's baseball teams and 14 women's softball teams were already playing a full schedule of league games on diamonds marked out in the camp's bulldozed firebreaks. A few teams, including the Dusty Chicks (above) arrived at Manzanar intact from their prewar neighborhoods. Games played on a regulation major league field with bleachers and a backstop drew thousands of spectators. As they cheered on the Yankees, the Scorpions, and other teams, internees could once more be part of an America they still believed in. Below, Bishop High School football players take time out from practice for a team photograph in 1915. (Above, War Relocation Authority photograph, National Archives, NWDS-210-G-D527.)

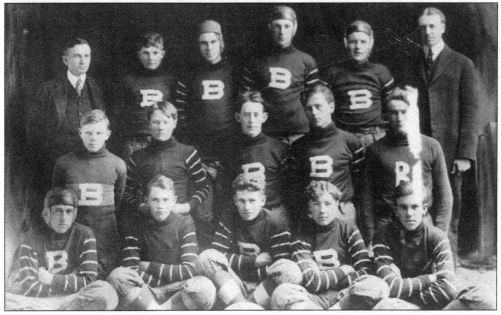

Organized in 1941 by Lone Pine ranchers Russell Spainhower and Wilfred Cline, the Lone Pine Stampede celebrated southern Inyo's cowboy and ranching heritage every Memorial Day weekend for more than 25 years. Visitors and townspeople joined in the Wild West atmosphere, as top riders appeared at the professional rodeo, local girls vied to be stampede queen, and the popular parade, burro races, whiskerino contest, and barbecue rounded out the program.

Aviator Silas Christofferson is seen here with his tractor biplane at the Bishop fairground in 1914. The aviation exhibition, sponsored by the Inyo Good Road Club, drew large crowds and generated much excitement. For many spectators, it was their first view of a "flying machine." Another cheering crowd watched a few days later as Christofferson flew from Lone Pine over Mount Whitney, breaking the American altitude record.

Homes in the Owens Valley came in many sizes and forms, from traditional Paiute shelters to modest farm homes and ornate Victorian mansions. The families who lived in them were often large, and the descendants of many pioneer families still live in the valley. Members of the McGovern family are seen above at their ranch at George's Creek around 1910, with pioneers Augustus and Annie McGovern holding their young grandchildren. Below, the large extended family of Big Pine resident Joseph Freeman Chrysler and his wife, Cynthia Jane, has gathered on July 4, 1909, at the Big Pine home of Thomas Tate.

Owens Valley residents take advantage of their proximity to the Sierra Nevada's high-elevation meadows and the rugged canyons of the White-Inyo Mountains, where beauty and solitude have always been just a short drive, hike, or horseback ride away. These Independence residents are enjoying the splendor of their alpine backyard around 1928. The Sierras' eastern slopes became part of the Inyo National Forest, established by Pres. Theodore Roosevelt in 1907; the forest now encompasses over 2.1 million acres of land in the Sierra Nevada and White-Inyo Mountains, much of it bordering the Owens Valley on both sides. Today, more than four million visitors use the forest in a typical year. In 1924, recreational users numbered just over 67,000, of which 55,500 were campers. Local residents were often among them, heading to higher elevations to escape the valley's summertime heat. Most people set up camp near a wagon or automobile, needed to transport heavy canvas tents, cots, and cooking gear. Only the hardiest mountain explorers carried their gear in packs and traveled on foot. (Thomas Poole collection.)

National Park Service ranger Carrie Andresen-Strawn leads a tour at Manzanar National Historic Site in May 2012. A significant government presence has been part of Owens Valley life since the US Army established Camp Independence in 1862. Today, 98 percent of Inyo County land is owned by federal, state, or city government agencies and their employees account for more than one-third of the county's labor force. (Manzanar National Historic Site.)

Born in the Owens Valley about 1856, Emma Earl Symmes and her family were among the nearly 1,000 Paiute removed to Fort Tejon in 1863. They escaped and returned to the valley, and she later lived at Fort Independence. Symmes became an accomplished basket weaver, and like many Paiute women, did housework and took care of children for white families. She is seen here about 1930 in Independence with Charles and Betty Haines, the children of her longtime employer.

Presiding as Inyo County Superior Court judge from 1908 until his death in 1949, William P. Dehy (pictured) was a respected friend of Inyo County, both on the bench and off. Raised on a ranch near Bishop, he taught school at Fish Springs before earning a degree at Hastings College of the Law in San Francisco. When asked to issue arrest warrants for leaders of the November 1924 aqueduct takeover at the Alabama Spillway, Judge Dehy disqualified himself "for personal interest." Below, the Commander's House, an iconic Independence landmark and symbol of the valley's pioneer past, is seen in a recent watercolor rendering by Independence artist Susan Holgate. The house was brought from the former Fort Independence military post in the late 1800s and rebuilt on Edwards Street (US Highway 395). (Below, Susan Holgate painting.)

Inyo County's fourth and present courthouse (above) "would be a credit to a much larger county," newspaperman W.A. Chalfant wrote soon after the building's completion in 1921. Now in the National Register of Historic Places, the Neoclassical Revival structure, the only one of its kind in the Eastern Sierra, holds county offices and one large courtroom, and it still houses the county library in part of the basement. At its dedication on April 10, 1922, according to the *Inyo Independent*, "uncertain weather conditions" limited attendance to 700 people, but with judge William Dehy presiding, they enjoyed a historical pageant and selections by the Fort Independence Indian Band and Owens Valley High School Glee Club. Speeches from California governor William Stephens and other dignitaries followed. Vehicles line Edwards Street in Independence on dedication day, with the Inyo County Jail on the left (below).

Salty-tongued Dr. Irving Woodin (above) left a fashionable New York medical practice and came west after contracting tuberculosis. He soon recovered in the dry desert air and then took on medical care for the southern Owens Valley, traveling between Independence and Keeler in a sagging buggy, and later in this automobile, seen in 1915 at Keeler. Those needing the doctor signaled with a white rag tied to a gate or crossroads post. Though reportedly fond of drink, "Doc" Woodin was a devoted doctor and a trusted friend, and he rarely collected payment unless he was short of cash. Below, before the first building of Northern Inyo Hospital was completed in 1949, Bishop medical facilities, including the Bishop Hospital, were often in homes rented from the City of Los Angeles after it bought residential property in the early 1930s. (Laws Museum and Historic Site.)

Lillian Linde Hilderman arrived in the Owens Valley in 1909 from Minnesota. She worked first as a nurse for Dr. Irving Woodin and was later appointed Keeler's postmaster. Her weekly Keeler columns in the Chalfant Press newspapers, with their homespun reporting and unique writing style, were reader favorites. Once a popular feature in the local press, town columns kept readers updated on bridge parties and baby showers and reported on residents' travels and visitors. Few events escaped Lillian's notice; she notes in one column that "Andy Pedneau fell out of bed Wednesday night. Doctor's attention received Thursday a.m." Reporting on railroad activity at the narrow gauge station across the street from the post office, she writes, "Regular passenger went out on train Tuesday, ticket and everything." Lillian Hilderman lived in Keeler until her death in 1976 at age 89. (Right, author's collection.)

Cattle and tule elk are often seen in the same fields near US Highway 395 south of Big Pine. Found only in California, tule elk were nearing extinction in their native San Joaquin Valley when local residents sponsored the introduction of 55 elk into the Owens Valley in 1933–1934. With careful management, the population has grown to include six herds between Owens Lake and Bishop. (Author's collection.)

Cattle from Lone Pine's Anchor Ranch are moved to desert grazing at Ash Creek in March 2010. Early in the summer each year, they are driven to summer range at Monache Meadow in the Sierra south of Lone Pine. Livestock production has remained vital to the Owens Valley economy for more than 150 years; in 2011, there were more than 24,000 cattle and sheep, valued at $24 million, in Inyo County. (Michael Pietrobon photograph.)

Seven

INSPIRED

Legendary mountaineer and scholar Norman Clyde (1885–1972) lived much of his extraordinary life in the Sierra Nevada backcountry, logging more than 100 first ascents, leading climbing expeditions, and locating downed aircraft and missing hikers. He lived from a huge pack filled with food, cooking equipment, and books in Greek and Latin. In the 1920s, he was the high school principal in Independence; today, his legacy inspires new generations of mountaineers.

Young author Mary Austin yearned to write about the desert landscape and the people she encountered after moving to the Owens Valley in 1892, but financial and marital strains and a mentally impaired daughter sapped her health and spirit. She taught school in Lone Pine and Bishop and, in 1900, settled in Independence in "the brown house under the willow tree" where she wrote her 1903 classic *The Land of Little Rain*. In it, she describes "My Neighbor's Field," an expanse of desert scrub visible beyond her home (below). "The field [was] not greatly esteemed of the town," she notes. She, too, endured the scorn of townspeople for her outspoken manner, feminist views, and friendships with Paiute and Mexican families. After leaving Independence in 1905, she wrote more than 30 books, many inspired by the Owens Valley.

With a camera lens concealed in his luggage, Los Angeles photographer Toyo Miyatake entered the Manzanar "reception center" in 1942 and, against regulations, began fulfilling a self-described "historic duty" to record life in camp. He worked in secret for several months before being discovered and was eventually permitted to photograph without restrictions. He produced some 1,500 images of Manzanar, including this barracks view with 14,375-foot Mount Williamson in the background. (Toyo Miyatake Photograph, Toyo Miyatake Studio.)

Captivated by the Owens Valley's landscape and flora, Independence resident Mary DeDecker taught herself botany and became the preeminent authority on Inyo plant life. A new genus of the buckwheat family she discovered carries her name: *Dedekera eurekensis* (July gold). As a founding member of the Owens Valley Committee, she lent her expertise and advocated tirelessly for a long-term water agreement with Los Angeles. (Bristlecone Chapter, California Native Plant Society.)

Electrical pioneer L.L. Nunn's bold vision of higher education has guided Deep Springs College since its founding in 1917 on 1,800 acres of isolated high desert east of Big Pine. The college's "three pillars"—rigorous academics, labor, and self-governance—help prepare 26 students "of exceptional promise" for lives of "leadership and enlightened service" in their chosen fields. Most continue on to prestigious universities and advanced degrees. The two-year program emphasizes political deliberation and accountability to the community. Students operate a cattle ranch, alfalfa farm, and dairy, making the college largely self-sustaining. Above, Nunn (third row, center, with glasses) is seen with students and faculty in 1922. Below, a student dairyman delivers fresh milk to the kitchen in 1926. (Both, Deep Springs College Archive.)

All Paiute girls learned to weave the everyday willow baskets once used for storage, transport, cooking, and cradling infants. Today, those simple baskets tell the story of a lost way of life and are reminders of their weavers' unique connections with the natural world. As modern containers replaced baskets, expert Paiute and Panamint Shoshone weavers produced more of the decorative baskets known as "made-for-sale" baskets, with animals, birds, and insects woven into their designs. Most were sold to tourists; others found their way into local white collections as gifts or payment for goods and services. Today, they are regarded as works of art. Panamint Shoshone weaver Isabel Hanson, seen at right in 1963, lived in the Darwin area and reportedly wove every day. The collection of Bishop educator Minnie Barrows Randolph is seen below in 1911.

Three seasons of summer concerts, from 1965 to 1968, attracted nationally known artists to the Deepest Valley Theatre. Founded by author Evelyn Eaton, it occupied a natural amphitheater formed by the Alabama Hills' dramatic granite outcroppings. Among the featured performers was Iren Marik, a Hungarian-born concert pianist and former student of Béla Bartók. After defecting to the United States after World War II, she later settled in Independence and gave informal monthly concerts in her home.

Educator and historian Dorothy Clora Cragen speaks at the dedication of the new Eastern California Museum building in May 1968. Following 16 years as the Inyo County superintendent of schools, she became museum director. During her tenure, Cragen increased preservation efforts and secured the land and funding for the new museum. Through her writings, lectures, and field trips, she promoted awareness of the valley's rich historical heritage.

As interest in radio astronomy grew worldwide following World War II, the California Institute of Technology established the Owens Valley Radio Observatory on a 300-acre site near Big Pine. The valley's sparse population, isolation, and flat, open spaces provide optimal conditions and minimal radio interference for the project. In 1956, Caltech scientists and graduate students began on-site construction of two 90-foot radio telescopes, seen here on December 19, 1958, when they were dedicated. The huge telescopes, together called an interferometer, were then the most sensitive in existence and were used to gather information on the nature of distant radio galaxies. Scientists added a 130-foot antenna to the site in 1968, and, in the 1970s, modified the original 90-foot installations for use in mapping the galaxy and for studies of solar physics. More recent work has included the Combined Array for Research in Millimeter-wave Astronomy, an array of smaller antennas now installed at the high-elevation Cedar Flat site nearby. Scientists, graduate researchers, and other personnel who work at the facility live mainly in Bishop. (California Institute of Technology Archive.)

Native son Robert Symons, seen here in a glider above Bishop, had twin passions: flying and the Sierra Nevada. He became an internationally-recognized soaring pioneer, and closer to home, was known as a mountain pilot without equal. Operating the Bishop Flying Service, he flew hundreds of search and rescue, aerial photography, and snow survey operations. His pioneering Sierra cloud-seeding program, flown in a converted P-38, drew national attention. Intrigued by the lenticular clouds seen over the Owens Valley during strong ground winds, he collected data during hundreds of flights in gliders and powered aircraft, many in dangerous updraft conditions of the little-understood mountain lee waves. His meticulous observations contributed to knowledge of the wave phenomenon and led to the Sierra Wave Project, which brought world-renowned scientists and pilots to Bishop and established the Owens Valley as a soaring mecca. In 1951, Symons set a world altitude record of 38,305 feet in a two-place glider. After his death in a glider accident in 1958, the California senate adjourned in his memory, and Bishop honored its friend and former city councilman with the largest funeral in its history. (Patricia Symons Rowbottom collection.)

Eight
A ROAD RUNS
THROUGH IT

The Owens Valley's iconic north-south artery, US Highway 395, is seen in this 2004 photograph looking south near the former Manzanar War Relocation Center site. It was later rerouted to its present location to the east. Formerly part of the El Camino Sierra state highway between Mojave and Bridgeport, it was designated a federal highway in 1934 and became part of the Three Flags Highway between Mexico and Canada. (Author's collection.)

The Inyo County Wagon Road passes through Lone Pine in this 1874 photograph, the earliest known image of the town. By then, wood-frame construction had replaced the original adobe structures, leveled in the earthquake two years before. During periods of high spring runoff, mountain streams such as Lone Pine Creek, in the foreground, branched and flowed unchecked across roads and through towns.

A pack train heading south kicks up dust on the unpaved highway through Independence, about 1927. Town water wagons helped control the dust, but business owners celebrated when hard surfacing of El Camino Sierra, "the mountain highway," was completed between Mojave and Bishop in 1931. The flagpole that stood at the intersection with Market Street was removed before paving. (Author's collection.)

The winter of 1933 saw a month of nearly continuous snowfall that brought most travel between towns to a halt, stranding residents and livestock alike. Here, sheep are being driven south through Big Pine to escape the dangerous conditions. (Bruce Branson collection.)

The snow removal equipment available at the time was no match for the nearly five feet of accumulated snow on Main Street in Bishop during the January 1933 storms. Residents took to skis and wagons to get around, and at least one merchant brought a horse-drawn sleigh out of retirement to make deliveries.

In the arid Owens Valley, severe storms could turn unpaved roads into quagmires. Above, the road through Big Pine is flooded after heavy rains on January 25, 1914. Below, today's US Highway 395 is still vulnerable to closure, but now with the added potential for traffic tie-ups. Near Independence, a torrent of water and mud unleashed by a fierce thunderstorm on July 12, 2008, washed down canyons and across scrubland burned in a wildfire the previous summer. It destroyed the historic Bright ranch and other homes and buried thousands of fish at the Mount Whitney Hatchery. Mud, boulders, and debris covered the four-lane highway for several hundred yards, backing up vacation traffic in both directions. California Highway Patrol vehicles are seen escorting travelers through the mudflow the next morning. (Below, Ken Babione photograph.)

Developer George Chaffey's plans for the 1910 Manzanar fruit-growing subdivision included replacing the old wagon road with a "broad, straight road" that would connect the new town of Manzanar to Independence, six miles north. Called Independence Avenue, it was later incorporated into El Camino Sierra and US Highway 395. Seen above in 1912, Manzanar's community hall and general store stood along the road's west side. Below, a six-mile-long caravan of 200 or more private vehicles, driven by their Japanese American owners and accompanied by military trucks and jeeps, turns off the highway into the half-finished "Owens Valley Reception Center" at Manzanar on March 23, 1942. The first to arrive, these internees helped set up medical, kitchen, and other facilities for the thousands soon to follow. The US Army permanently impounded the internees' vehicles. (Below, Merritt Collection, Eastern California Museum.)

Little Lake's namesake spring-fed lake, first called Little Owens Lake, is a haven for migrating birds. A natural resting place for travelers as well, the area was an early stage way station and later a stop on the Southern Pacific line from Mojave to the Owens Valley. In 1923, Bill and Elvira Bramlette built the landmark Little Lake Hotel, store, and garage. Weary automobile travelers could spend a night or find water for overheated vehicles. Below, the geothermal springs at Coso, considered a place of healing by Native Americans, lie east of the highway, north of Little Lake. Now within the restricted China Lake Naval Air Weapons Station, the area was commercialized in the 1920s and 1930s with a hotel and a bathhouse. Visitors could buy bottled Coso mineral water and Coso Mud, a beauty aid made from the clay surrounding the springs.

Photographer Gordon Hastings snapped these travelers who stopped along the highway north of Lone Pine in 1940 to look at Mount Whitney, the highest point in the contiguous United States. Set back in the Sierra range, it appears lower than other, closer peaks. Hastings, a driver for Warner Bros. Studios, was in Lone Pine for the filming at Whitney Portal of *High Sierra* starring Humphrey Bogart. (Gordon Hastings collection.)

Built in 1930 on highway frontage leased from the Lacey Ranch, Olancha's Farm House Café has operated continuously ever since. Managers Dick and Alberta Hiter changed the name in 1938 and advertised with postcards that were popular at the time. Set amid the giant cottonwood trees that have lined the highway through Olancha for more than a century, today's Ranch House Café is still a "good place to eat." (Bruce Branson collection.)

Travel on the rutted, unpaved El Camino Sierra in the 1920s was a challenge for early motorists and their vehicles, as they encountered flooding, dust storms, wildlife, and wandering livestock, as well as inebriated and speeding drivers. As an oncoming car approached, both vehicles had to move to the side to pass, leaving their left wheels in the deep tire ruts. As the largest town at the Owens Valley's southern end, Lone Pine has always offered travelers a wide choice of restaurants, gas stations, and lodging options. Carl Bruno's Square Deal Station, seen above in 1924, provided towing and repair service to help get drivers back on the road. Below, Ellis Motors opened a glistening new Shell station in 1941, complete with white-uniformed attendants.

By 1927, El Camino Sierra through the Owens Valley was part of the state highway system. Traffic increased as fishermen from around the state discovered the Eastern Sierra's lakes and streams, and more Owens Valley residents became the proud owners of automobiles. Established in 1930, the California Highway Patrol (CHP) was charged with enforcing "traffic laws on county and State highways." On February 9 of that year, it organized an Inyo County unit, with headquarters in Independence and five officers. Seen in this Allan Ramsey portrait, they are, from left to right, Leroy Roeper, Rollin Bell, Capt. Otto Buer, Oscar McMurry, and James Ford. Later assigned to San Bernardino, Officer McMurry died in 1934 from injuries received in the line of duty and is among the earliest of the CHP's honored "Fallen Heroes."

Above, Independence residents welcome the Highway Post Office bus on its inaugural run through the Owens Valley on July 14, 1952. The bus is stopped at the Independence Post Office, located then in the Pines Café building. With rail traffic declining nationwide, the big red, white, and blue buses of the Highway Post Office service were a familiar sight on rural highways during the 1950s. Outfitted inside like the railroad mail cars they replaced, the buses followed routes averaging 150 miles each way to eliminate time-consuming refueling stops. Below, mules pull a wagon loaded with aqueduct construction equipment through Independence about 1910.

US Highway 395 is both a fast-moving thoroughfare between Los Angeles and Reno and a reduced-speed-limit Main Street for the Owens Valley's communities. Town parades celebrate history, heritage, and local identity and are social events as well. When the Big Pine Community Band played in Bishop's Harvest Festival parade in 1912 (above), horse-drawn traffic moved alongside the marchers at about the same pace. During today's parades, vacationers and other travelers are diverted around the processions and through the quiet side streets of Bishop, Big Pine, Independence, and Lone Pine. Mules pull a prospector's wagon in the 2009 Bishop Mule Days parade (below). Started in 1969 by Eastern Sierra packers, the five-day salute to mules in the region's history features competitive mule shows and brings an estimated 20,000 visitors to Bishop each Memorial Day weekend. (Below, author's collection.)

Bishop residents welcome racecar driver William W. "Bill" Bramlette at the end of his trip from Los Angeles in a record-setting eight hours and 18 minutes on March 12, 1921. A well-known road racer, Bramlette later settled in the Owens Valley and built the Little Lake Hotel. On April 19, 1921, race driver E.T. Conners bested Bramlette's time by 44 minutes, making the 288-mile trip in seven hours and 18 minutes.

The steep grade of Sherwin Hill rises from Round Valley and marks the Owens Valley's northern boundary. A 10-mile stretch of graded highway completed in 1916 replaced the wagon road built in 1870 by pioneer James Sherwin and opened the Owens Valley to automobile travel to and from the north. In this 1920s view from Sherwin grade, majestic Mount Tom towers above as the road winds out of the valley.

BIBLIOGRAPHY

Austin, Mary. *The Land of Little Rain*. Boston: Houghton Mifflin, 1903.

Belden, L. Burr and Mary DeDecker. *Death Valley to Yosemite: Frontier Mining Camps and Ghost Towns*. Bishop, CA: Spotted Dog Press, 2000.

Brooks, Joan. *Desert Padre: The Life and Writings of Father John J. Crowley, 1881–1940*. Desert Hot Springs, CA: Mesquite Press, 1997.

Chalfant, W.A. *The Story of Inyo*. Rev. ed. Bishop, CA: Chalfant Press, 1933.

Dean, Sharon E., Peggy S. Ratcheson, Judith W. Finger, and Ellen F. Daus. *Weaving a Legacy: Indian Baskets and the People of Owens Valley, California*. Salt Lake City: University of Utah Press, 2004.

Eastern California Museum, Independence. www.inyocounty.us/ecmuseum.

Hoffman, Abraham. *Vision or Villainy: Origins of the Owens Valley Water Controversy*. College Station: Texas A&M University Press, 1981.

Houston, Jeanne Watkasuki and James D. Houston. *Farewell to Manzanar: A True Story of Japanese American Experience During and After the World War II Internment*. Boston: Houghton Mifflin, 1973.

Irwin, Sue. *California's Eastern Sierra: A Visitor's Guide*. Los Olivos, CA: Cachuma Press, 1991.

Nadeau, Remi. *The Water Seekers*. Garden City, NY: Doubleday, 1950.

Putnam, Jeff and Genny Smith. *Deepest Valley: Guide to Owens Valley, Its Roadsides and Mountain Trails*. Rev. ed. Mammoth Lakes, CA: Genny Smith Books, 1995.

Turner, George. *Slim Rails Through the Sand*. Los Angeles: Trans-Anglo Books, 1964.

Walton, John. *Western Times and Water Wars: State, Culture, and Rebellion in California*. Berkeley: University of California Press, 1992.

Wehrey, Jane. *Voices From This Long Brown Land: Oral Recollections of Owens Valley Lives and Manzanar Pasts*. New York: Palgrave Macmillan, 2006.

Visit us at
arcadiapublishing.com

CPSIA information can be obtained
at www.ICGtesting.com
Printed in the USA
BVHW092002130721
611837BV00003B/530